Improving Comprehension
with
Think-Aloud Strategies

BY JEFFREY D. WILHELM

S C H O L A S T I C
PROFESSIONAL**B**OOKS

NEW YORK · TORONTO · LONDON · AUCKLAND · SYDNEY
MEXICO CITY · NEW DELHI · HONG KONG · BUENOS AIRES

Dedication

To Theresa McMannus, who, like all good teachers, helps others to do their work.
And to all of you who are dedicated to the art of teaching.

Cover concept by Kathy Massaro
Cover design by Kelli Thompson and Vitomir Zarkovic
Cover photo by Michael C. York
Interior photos on pages 41, 93, 101, 105, 108, 114, 121, 127, 146, 160, 161 by Michael C. York; on pages 138 and 154 by Vicki Kasala; all other by Wendy Murray
Illustration on page 17 by Antonio Castro
Illustration on page 173 by Gil, courtesy of Attic Studios
Interior design by LDL Designs

ISBN 0-439-21859-4
Copyright © 2001 by Jeffrey D. Wilhelm
All rights reserved.
Printed in the U.S.A.

Table of Contents

Acknowledgments

In college I had a Bible professor who wrote thank-you notes each November to people to whom he was grateful. He recommended it as a profoundly salutary and humbling pursuit. You could write a letter a day and never run out of folks to whom you feel grateful, he told me. He also said that almost everyone on your list, if not everyone, would be someone who had been your teacher. He meant both the teachers we have in schools and the teachers we meet throughout our lives: those who teach us by example, who lend us a hand when we need it, who mentor us through friendship and loving-kindness.

I've engaged in this project a few times, and my professor was right: Everyone I wrote to was and often continues to be a teacher to me. The process makes me feel connected to the world in a way I don't always feel. I realize that there are many people who have contributed to my development, encouraging me and helping me refine my thinking and my skills in varied pursuits, from teaching and research to cooking, kayaking, carpentry, and raising a family. It's humbling to engage in a project such as writing this book and to realize how many people have contributed, and recognize that I can't thank them all without filling up many more pages than are reasonably allowed for acknowledgments. So let me begin by expressing gratitude to my teachers.

First, my wife, Peggy Jo, and my daughters, Fiona Luray and Jasmine Marie, and my father, Jack Wilhelm. I need always to thank my friend and mentor Michael Smith for his constant guidance and patience. I thank George Hillocks and Bruce Novak for all they have taught me about teaching.

Theresa McMannus and Gail Garthwait deserve special thanks for their daily helpfulness. I'd like to thank coauthors on previous books, such as Tanya Baker and Julie Dube, and my old team-teaching partner Paul Friedemann. I learned so much from working with you! Huge dosages of appreciation are deserved by friends and teaching colleagues like Brian Ambrosius, Bill Anthony, Deb Appleman, Jim Artesani, Rosemary Bamford, Erv Barnes, Bill Bedford, Kylene Beers, Jim Blaser, Ed Brazee, Jim Chiavacci, Paul Corrigan, Mike Ford, Stuart Greene, Leon Holley Jr., Bruce Hunter, Rich Kent, Jan Kristo, Craig Martin, Bruce Nelson, Wayne Otto, Brenda Power, Bill Strohm, Brian White, and Denny Wolfe. Thanks to my dean, Robert Cobb, my supporter, Kay Hyatt, and all of the former and current fellows in the Maine Writing Project—and many others too numerous to mention. Thank you!

Thanks, of course, to my editor, Wendy Murray, who has helped to create and shape this project with her insightful editing and care.

And again, I'd like to thank everyone who is a teacher. Without you, well, there would be no learning! I am eager to continue learning from you. If you use ideas in these books, adapt or elaborate on them in particular ways that you find successful, I'd be most gratified to hear and learn from you. I can be reached by e-mail at Jeff_Wilhelm@umit.maine.edu.

Foreword

Some people I know—not many, just some—sincerely try to practice what they preach. It's an admirable trait, and I know from personal observation that Jeff Wilhelm has it. What Jeff tells us in *Improving Comprehension with Think-Aloud Strategies* is what he does with real students in real classrooms. But that's only part of the story. Jeff turns the old adage around and does a fine job of preaching what he practices too. He shares what he has learned from years of thoughtful practice in a straightforward, accessible style. Jeff not only tells us what he does, he takes us through the steps that will enable us to do it too.

It would have been great if my dad, a Chevy mechanic, had turned the adage around. Pa preached the well-tuned engine, and he tuned engines well. But now, every time I take my car in for a $70 an hour tune-up, I wish that he'd told me *how*. Jeff tells us how.

Once in a while Pa did try to share some of his engine-tuning expertise with me, but I never did get past the part where you "take off that cap and pour the oil in there." Both Pa and I were inclined to blame my short attention span for my lack of understanding, but Jeff reminds us that there probably is a better explanation: Pa's expertise and advice were outside my **zone of proximal development.** So when Pa was connecting the gizmo to the whatsis, I was still trying to figure out which was which, why he turned one clockwise and the other counterclockwise, and how he managed to get hold of either of them without banging into the frimfram that seemed to be in the way. Pa told me what, but he never told me how. In spite of good intentions, the expert (Pa) didn't take note of the novice's (my) hang-ups, so these days the novice is paying seventy bucks an hour for tune-ups that he might have learned to do himself.

Good intentions and expertise are necessary but not sufficient to assure successful learning. As Jeff points out, the tradition among well intentioned, knowledgeable teachers has been to focus on the transfer of information (what), but to neglect sharing the strategies (how) that can enable students to make effective use of newly acquired information. In *Improving Comprehension with Think-Aloud Strategies,* and in the books to come in the series *Action Strategies for Readers,* he shows us how we teachers can do a more effective job of sharing our expertise with novice students.

The think-aloud strategies presented in this book have evolved from ideas formulated by Russian psychologist Lev Vygotsky. Each child, he said, has a **zone of actual development** (ZAD), where she can operate effectively without assistance. (So when Pa and I turned to tuning the engine of my '55 Chevy, my ZAD was at the level of "taking off that cap and pouring the oil in there.") Vygotsky went on to suggest that effective learning can proceed only if the task at hand is in the learner's **zone of proximal development** (ZPD). At that level the learner cannot handle the task alone, but he can tackle it successfully with the help of a more expert person. (I never learned much about engine tuning because I didn't understand the terminology or how to handle the tools. Pa's demonstrations were beyond my ZPD.)

The Think-Aloud strategies that Jeff presents enable teachers to zero in on a student's ZPD and to determine precisely where help is needed. And he doesn't let us forget Vygotsky's admonition that "the teacher must first generously model how to work through a task, highlighting and naming how a particular strategy or strategies can be used to successfully complete it." And then, of course, the student is given opportunities to try the strategy with various levels of assistance. Learning proceeds as a two-sided process, with both the teacher and the student involved all along the way: The expert notices what the novice understands and helps the novice where needed to move forward.

I can't help but wonder what might have come to pass if Jeff had been there when Pa and I were tuning my Chevy. Who knows? I might have wound up on one of the pit crews at the Indy 500!

—Wayne Otto
Emeritus Professor of Curriculum and Instruction, University of Wisconsin

The Thinking Behind Think-Alouds

This book is the first in a series entitled *Action Strategies for Readers.* The premise behind it is simple: the most important thing we can teach our students is how to learn. Or put another way, the most powerful thing we can teach is strategic knowledge, a knowledge of the procedures people use to learn, to think, to read, and to write. The most effective way to introduce students to how to use these tools is to model them in the contexts of meaningful tasks and then to assist students in their own use of these strategies.

For our purposes, this means that to help our students to become expert readers, we must model the strategies of expert readers using authentic texts—novels, short stories, non-fiction books, newspaper articles, arguments, and Internet sites—and then support students in taking on these expert stances for themselves as they read independently.

Though this idea may seem obvious, it stands in direct contrast to the theories and practices that dominate most of American curriculum, instruction, and testing. Reviews of American education show that we spend most of our time teaching students information, filling them with declarative knowledge (the *what),* instead of assisting them to enact new and more proficient ways of reading, problem solving, and making meaning (the *how).*

This is unfortunate, as the research clearly shows that when students are asked to learn information without actively using procedures to construct understanding, they usually end up forgetting the *what*—the content. Never having learned the how, they are put squarely behind the eight ball and do not know how to learn on their own.

The Action Strategies series will attempt to help turn this deep-seated trend around. With each book, I'll show you how to help students learn *ways of reading.* Some of these ways, called general-process strategies, can be applied to any type of text or content they encounter. Other strategies, known as task or text specific processes, are necessary to comprehending particular text conventions or genres. As our students read and solve problems and inquire using these strategies, they will of course also deeply learn content.

Each book in this series will introduce a family of teaching strategies for assisting students to learn reading strategies. The teaching technique highlighted in this book is a think-aloud, in which a reader makes his reading process manifest to others by articulating all that he is noticing, thinking, feeling, and doing as he reads a text.

Vygotsky's Two-Sided Model of Teaching and Learning

The teaching/learning theories of noted Russian psychologist Lev Vygotsky and his followers inform many of the ideas you will encounter in this book and the subsequent ones in this series. Vygotsky's theories have been hugely influential on successful early-literacy programs like Reading Recovery® and Guided Reading, and his ideas are just beginning to gain a foothold in instruction for older students.

Vygotsky and neo-Vygotskians build their ideas on the premise that *what is learned must be taught*. Sounds simple enough, but as you will see when you read about the three basic models of teaching and learning influential today, most schools and much classroom activity runs counter to this notion and fails to fully understand what it means to teach.

The most prevalent teaching/learning model today is the teacher/information–centered model, in which teaching is the purveying of information (this model transforms the old saw "those who can't do, teach," to "those who can tell, teach"). This is considered a one-sided model because learning is centered on the information possessed by the teacher, which flows one way, from the teacher to the student.

A reaction against this model is the progressive student-centered model, in which the student learns about an interest of his choice. The teacher provides a nurturing environment for student exploration and discovery. This is also considered a one-sided model because learning is driven by the student (i.e., "those who can get kids to articulate and pursue their own interests, teach").

The third is a two-sided learning-centered model in which expertise is given over to students in an exchange ("those who can do something, understand how to do that something, and can assist others to do it, teach"). This model stands in direct contrast to the prevailing one-sided teacher, information-centered model. In this model, the teacher teaches through the relationship cultivated with a student in the context of working together closely. It goes well beyond the one-sided student-centered model in which students construct their own understandings in a nurturing environment but without the direct interventions of the teacher. In the learning-centered model, expertise is explicitly and continuously shared with the student as teacher and student engage together in meaningful and productive shared activities.

I've always questioned the teacher-centered model because it focuses on *what* but not *how*. Research in cognitive science has made it compellingly clear that just telling students information is a weak form of teaching. Though the student-centered model is a major improvement over the teacher-centered model, I critique it too, because this model assumes that much learning occurs naturally. Given the conventionality of texts (i.e., given that texts are constructed in certain ways not because of nature but because people have agreed to construct and read them in certain ways), I do not believe that we learn to read naturally. A child locked in a room with books would not learn to read them on her own; she needs someone to teach her how print works and what she is expected to do as a reader. I would also argue that the teacher who believes in natural learning often deprives the student of her full expertise as a reader.

And so I champion the two-sided learning-centered model based on Vygotsky: learning is the crucial element, and we recognize that teaching and learning are two sides of the same coin, two parts in the same dance.

Vygotsky's View of Reading

According to Vygotsky and his followers, we must learn ways of reading and thinking in order to participate fully in our culture and to make meaning within it; these ways have to be passed from experts to novices in the context of meaningful, collaborative activity. For them, a book is more than just words on a page or a narrative that will move us or inform us, it is a highly conventionalized form of language. Authors and readers use agreed-upon sets of conventions in order to convey meaning and make meaning, from knowing that quotation marks signal that a character is speaking to subtler codes signaling a character's intention or reliability. Teaching these conventions requires a more expert reader to notice what a novice reader understands and then assist him to a higher level of understanding. This is teaching because it actively assists and promotes growth. Think-alouds are a powerful way to teach because they give students the expert's keys to unlock a text's fullest construction of meaning.

Vygotsky's Zones

Vygotsky maintained that every child has a cognitive *zone of actual development* (ZAD). This zone is defined by what the child can do on her own without any kind of assistance. Vygotsky believed that if you give a child a task, like reading a book, and he does it, then you have taught him nothing. The child could already do the task, as that task was in his current zone of actual development.

Further, Vygotsky said that if you give a child a task to do and he cannot do it, then you have the chance to teach. If the child cannot do the task alone but can do it with a more expert person's help, then the task lies in what Vygotsky calls the *zone of proximal development* (ZDP). In this zone, students can do with help what they cannot do alone. Vygotsky argued that we can teach students something new only when the task is within their zone of proximal development.

What's the end goal? A classroom full of independent, engaged readers.

You'll see an example of "teaching in the zone" in Chapter 1 (page 21) as I use a think-aloud to teach a student named Josh. Josh could identify and discuss the literal details of Walter Dean Myers' novel *Monster*, but he could not make the inferences needed to fully comprehend the text. Understanding the directly stated details was within his zone of actual development; making even simple inferences was within his zone of proximal development (ZPD).

The think-aloud made the strategy of inferring tangible to Josh, putting it in a concrete form that he could study, consider, and respond to. This supports Vygotsky's assertion that all learning proceeds from the concrete to the abstract, and from the visible and external to the internal. In the chart that follows, I provide an overview of Vygotsky's model of learning.

Vygotskian Perspective: Teacher/Student Interactions

Student Responsibility ➝ Teacher Responsibility ➝ Joint Responsibility ➝ Self Responsibility

Zone of Actual Development	*Zone of Proximal Development*			*New Zone of Actual Development*
What the student can do on her own unassisted	Assistance provided by more capable others: teacher or peer or environment: classroom structures and activities	Transition from other assistance to self-assistance	Assistance provided by the self	Internalization, automatization

SOCIAL SPEECH
• Adult uses language to model process
• Adult and student share language and activity

PRIVATE SPEECH
student uses for herself language that adults use to regulate behavior (self-control)

INNER SPEECH
The student's silent, abbreviated dialogue that she carries on with self that is the essence of conscious mental activity

private speech internalized and transformed to inner verbal thought (self-regulation)

Adapted from Wilhelm, Baker, and Dube, 2001

The Zones

Vygotsky's concept of cognitive learning zones is so critical to appreciating this book—and to effective teaching—that I recap it here:

Zone of Actual Development—Independence: When we give a student a task in the zone of actual development, the student can already independently complete the task and there is nothing new to be learned, though such tasks may build confidence and fluency (some researchers believe that up to half of school time is spent teaching things that most of the kids already know and can do). Reading inventories designate texts that students can comprehend on their own as being at the "independent" reading level. These are texts that students can understand without assistance and therefore reading such texts is in that child's zone of actual development.

Within the Zone of Proximal Development—Instruction and Learning Occurs: If we give students a task within their zone of proximal development, the opportunity for learning is there, provided we assist. With assistance (teaching), students can do things they could not do before. Learning will occur! We do it until we see that students can accomplish the task without help, until the skill has moved into their zone of actual development. Reading inventories designate texts that students can comprehend with expert assistance as being at the "instructional" reading level. At this level, students will be successful with instructional help. As students are provided with help to read texts at this level, they learn new strategies of reading and achieve understanding in how certain textual conventions and text structures work to make meaning. The child becomes a more expert and knowledgeable reader by being assisted through this zone.

Beyond the Zone of Proximal Development—Frustration: If we give students a task that is beyond the zone of proximal development, then it will be too hard no matter how much support we give (e.g., if we try to teach Shakespeare to students whose sight vocabulary is low and who have never read drama, with its alternating speakers, stage directions, and other special conventions, then they may not succeed with the text no matter how much help we provide). Reading inventories designate texts that a student cannot comprehend even with assistance as being at her "frustrational" reading level. These are texts that students cannot comprehend and that frustrate them, demonstrating that the text lies beyond the zone of proximal development.

ACTIVE TEACHING IN THE ZPD:
OFFERING EXPLANATION, MODELING, GUIDED PRACTICE

To teach in the zone of proximal development, Vygotsky says the teacher must first generously model how to work through a task, highlighting and naming how a particular strategy or strategies can be used to successfully complete it. Then the teacher needs to provide opportunities for students to try the strategy, with various levels of assistance. After modeling, a teacher would then have students work in small groups, so they can assist one another, and so that she can circulate among them, helping when students get stuck. As the teacher notes evidence of students using the strategy effectively, she then provides a task in which students who are ready can use the strategy unassisted. If a student has trouble, the teacher can move her back a step by having her work with a peer or with the teacher herself. She then looks for evidence that students can use the strategy completely on their own, applying it and adapting it to new learning tasks. For example, after teaching Josh the strategy of inferring using the novel *Monster,* (see page 21) I would watch to see that Josh used inferences when reading another novel, during a class discussion of an article on cloning in *Time for Kids,* or in his reading journal. In other words, I look to see that a student has internalized new strategic knowledge and uses it independently and automatically. I look to see that the strategy is within his ZAD. This is the goal of all teaching and learning: independence.

Six Recursive Steps of Explicit Instruction

Remember, modeling doesn't stop after you've introduced a strategy. Throughout this teaching process, lend kids your strategic knowledge through active modeling and by stating what you are attending to. Literacy researchers Taylor, Harris, Pearson, and Garcia (1995) identify six recursive steps that occur in this kind of explicit instruction. When you read about Josh in the next chapter, you can refer to this list to see how I went through each of these steps.

1. Teacher explains *what* a strategy consists of.
2. Teacher explains *why* this strategy is important.
3. Teacher explains *when* to use the strategy in actual reading (e.g., what to notice in a text that tips off the reader that this particular strategy should be used).
4. Teacher *models how* to perform the strategy in an actual context (e.g., by doing a

think-aloud using a real text) while students observe.

5. Teacher *guides learner practice.* Teachers and students work through several increasingly challenging examples of the strategy together using authentic texts. Teacher gradually releases responsibility to the students, allowing them to do what they are capable of on their own and intervening and supporting only when needed and only as much as is absolutely needed.

6. Students *independently use* the strategy as they pursue their own reading and projects.

DO AS I SAY—AND AS I DO!
The Steps of Passing Strategic Expertise to Students

TEACHER DOES/STUDENTS WATCH
STEP 1: MODELING OF STRATEGY

Teacher uses and talks about strategy through use of technique like think-alouds.

Student observes.

Teacher stresses what, why, and when of strategy use.

TEACHER DOES/STUDENTS HELP
STEP 2: APPRENTICESHIP OF USE

Teacher uses strategy.

Student talks about and help, identifying when and how strategy should be used.

STUDENTS DO/TEACHER HELPS
STEP 3: SCAFFOLDING STRATEGY USE

Students use and talk about strategy with help of scaffolding technique like think-alouds, usually in small groups.

Teacher observes, provides feedback, and helps as needed.

STUDENTS DO/TEACHER WATCHES
STEP 4: INDEPENDENT USE

Student independently uses strategy, demonstrating competence through techniques like think-alouds

Teacher observes and assesses; plans future instruction

Adapted from Wilhelm, Baker, and Dube, 2001

Vygotsky's take on learning is incredibly liberating. In his view, any child can learn the next more difficult strategy or concept if given supportive instruction. Children can and will learn, no matter the obstacles, if they are given the right help. If students are not progressing, Vygotsky would assert that the instruction has not been appropriate, thereby rejecting the view of Jean Piaget that the child may have plateaued in a particular developmental stage. George Hillocks' influential research (1995) uses classroom data to make the same case. He draws on Benjamin Bloom's (1976, 1985) research on human potential to argue that almost any child can and will learn given the right opportunities and instruction. This is a wonderful position for us to embrace: if we give our developing readers the right kinds of help then they can and will learn to be better readers.

This book and the others in this series are dedicated to this end: to help provide you with flexible techniques for giving the right kind of help to your students, assistance that will move them through the four steps of modeling, apprenticeship, scaffolded use, and independent use, so they can become confident, motivated, and engaged readers.

THE PLACE OF STRATEGY INSTRUCTION IN YOUR READING PROGRAM

In my previous books on teaching reading I've maintained that reading well is a potentially life-transforming pursuit because it allows us to outgrow ourselves and become more than we currently are. This can only happen for our students if we fully embrace the idea that good reading requires good teaching, and that the more reluctant the readers we teach, the better and more powerful our teaching must be. But as we teach our students, there are several things to remember so that strategy instruction isn't overemphasized to the point that it interferes with rather than supports engaged reading.

- Reading strategies are important only insofar as they assist readers to construct meaningful understandings of texts. With this level of comprehension, readers can respond to, converse with, and even resist the meanings the author seems to put forth.

- Teaching strategies are important only insofar as they assist readers to comprehend and respond to text. In other words, think-alouds are a useful teaching strategy when they help a reader through her zone of proximal development, assisting her to develop a particular strategy or set of strategies that she cannot yet use independently, and when these strategies help her to engage with a text important to her current purposes.

• Think-alouds, like any teaching strategy, are not appropriate when students already know how to use a featured reading strategy, when they do not have a need to use the strategy, or when the strategy is so complex that it lies beyond their zone of proximal development. Once a new strategy is mastered, the scaffolding should be removed so students can use what they have learned independently to engage with the text.

The teaching and grouping structures explored throughout this book can provide various levels of support to whole-class, small groups, or individuals. They will help you teach each student in his zone of proximal development. The key is to use the strategy instruction flexibly. For example, if students have a general need to know a strategy in the context of a unit or reading, then I will teach them as a whole group. Often, because my students read with widely differing abilities, I will flexibly group them for strategy instruction. When I have the time, I find it most effective to work with students one-on-one. This is particularly important when a student has a unique need or when others in the class have already learned the strategy. If you use a workshop approach or have inquiry stations in your classroom, such tutoring can easily take place within these structures.

Sometimes I use more able readers to tutor less able ones. I find that even able readers benefit from using think-alouds (both in the role of student and more expert peer) to name and consolidate their own current strategy use and to find ways of extending and elaborating on that use.

The bottom line: think-alouds are a means to an end—and that end is engaged and reflective reading. Use the technique flexibly to give power over to your student readers.

CHAPTER 1

SEEING READING:
Making Strategic Knowledge Visible and Available to Students

The think-aloud technique supports readers as they hit the sometimes-rough currents of the more difficult kinds of texts they face in upper elementary and middle school.

WHAT IS A THINK-ALOUD?

It was our first overnight whitewater canoe trip. My partner was my younger daughter, Jasmine, who at age eight is already a "hammerhead," whitewater parlance for a gutsy and proficient canoeist.

As we neared Little Falls on the St. Croix River we could hear the thunderous rumble of cascading rapids and see the water vapor rising from the horizon line of the river. These class III rapids would provide a real challenge to our abilities as a canoe team.

We pulled over to the western bank so we could scout out possible routes. I asked Jasmine to tell me her plans for this canoe run. I needed to see if she understood how to successfully approach this new challenge and to have the opportunity to correct or help her if she did not. It was also important because we needed to agree on what to do so we could work together.

"Okay, Pappy," she started, taking a deep breath, "I think we should go river left." I followed her pointing finger. "And hit the V between those two big rocks. We'll be okay till we hit those pillow rocks down below. I'll give you a right draw and you sweep on the left to get around them. Hmmm… Once we get around that we need to hit that lower V. I think we should eddy out behind the big rock and then peel out into the main current. Then it's easy and we have fun the rest of the way down!"

She looked at me to see what I thought.

"Mmmm. Good thinking," I agreed. "That strategy would work." Jasmine was using the language, commands, and strategies of canoeing to map out a good plan. By having her think-aloud, I was able to access and judge her ideas… and intervene in ways that might help.

"But that's pretty technical and there's not too much room for error. I think there is an easier way," I suggested.

"You mean over here on river right?"

"Yes," I nodded.

"It looks easy below, but what about the pillow rocks right here?" she asked, throwing a rock into the first drop of the river right below us where barely submerged rocks formed a wall all the way across the current.

"If we have enough momentum we'll make that drop to the right of this rock, punch over the wall of rocks, draw left around the big rock below, and then head to the main current and be golden. What do you think? What route would be best?"

Page

377

A few moments later we were blasting down Little Falls river right, yelling to each other the commands we had already rehearsed during our think-aloud: "Left draw!" "Right sweep!" and even an occasional "Yippee!"

The think-aloud had been a great rehearsal for successfully completing our challenge. We had so much fun—and both felt so competent—that Jasmine made me carry the canoe up the portage trail two times so we could put in more rapid runs!

I chose to describe a think-aloud from the "real world" to show that this talking-through of an endeavor is natural, is a central way we help ourselves achieve—by saying aloud new steps until they become a part of our "inner voice" of knowledge.

In the classroom, a think-aloud supports readers as they hit the sometimes-rough currents of the more difficult kinds of texts they begin to face in upper elementary and middle school. Just as my daughter Jasmine had to know the specific demands of that stretch of the St. Croix River to keep from capsizing, taking her cues from the shapes and positions of rocks, the eddies, and currents, a reader has to know the underlying conventions of a text in order to keep meaning afloat. Without understanding what an author expects us to notice—whether it's a novelist's clue in dialogue about a character's deceit or a scientist's textbook bar graph showing rising air pollution—comprehension cannot take place. Think-alouds allow all students to hear how others sleuth out and make sense of all these text clues so that they can recognize and adopt these strategies as their own.

Tracking the Trail of a Porpoise

So, a think-aloud of reading is creating a record, either through writing or talking aloud, of the strategic decision-making and interpretive processes of going through a text, reporting everything the reader is aware of noticing, doing, seeing, feeling, asking, and understanding as she reads. A think-aloud involves talking about the reading strategies you are using and the content of the piece you are reading.

However, it's wise to keep in mind that the report will be partial. Jasmine's canoeing think-aloud certainly

CONSIDER THIS

Imagine if Jasmine and I had headed down the river without knowing much about canoeing and without talking through our approach. We would have overturned. No wonder students "drown" when we hand them a textbook or a sophisticated novel and say, *Here, read this,* without giving them the tools, rehearsal, and practice to prepare them for successfully navigating it.

did not reveal all her thinking and feelings. Think-alouds are also inexact reproductions of a person's actual thinking about reading; no one can thoroughly and accurately capture all of what he sees in his mind's eye. For these reasons, a think-aloud has been described as allowing us "to track the trail of a porpoise" because it gives us glimpses into hidden activity, allowing us to infer what is happening below the surface of consciousness. This is an apt analogy, because reading well is a highly complex activity, and there's much about it we don't understand—and may never know. I think we teachers need to remind ourselves of that fact. Learning to read well is tough going. As my daughter Fiona said to me when she was beginning to read more challenging books on her own, "Reading can be fun, but it can also be very flustrating!"

What the Research Says

In their seminal text *Verbal Protocols of Reading*, Pressley and Afflerbach trace the use of think-alouds from the time of Aristotle and Plato as a way of revealing and studying processes of thinking. In the last century, think-alouds have been used to develop psychological theory, understand problem solving in physics, reveal student strategy use and improvement during particular instructional interventions on various tasks, and to explore multiple other processing tasks.

I learned about think-alouds from the research literature on reading, where this technique—usually referred to as protocols—has been very useful in opening a window to understanding the highly complex and largely invisible processes of readers, writers, scientists, and others at work. As Pressley and Afflerbach report, "the human achievement of reading has few if any equals." These authors also provide an overview of how protocol research has helped us to understand the incredible complexity of reading and how it might be taught, to diagnose reading difficulties, and to monitor student readers' strategy use. My own research (see, for example, Wilhelm, 1997) has explored how think-aloud protocols can be used not only as a research technique but as a powerful way to instruct and assist students to understand and use more complex processes of reading.

In fact, my colleagues Tanya Baker and Julie Dube and I found that a major reason students struggle as readers in late elementary and middle school is because teachers underestimate the difficulty of the texts they are asking their students to read, including sophisticated narratives and expository texts, and therefore fail to provide the necessary assistance to help them successfully read these texts (Wilhelm, Baker, and Dube, 2001).

A Think-Aloud in Action: Helping Josh Infer

Here's an example of how think-alouds help me to assess and then assist a student who is having trouble. I was working with Josh, a lively sixth grader who, along with the rest of the class, was independently reading Walter Dean Myers' young-adult novel *Monster*. In this book, a young man named Steve Harmon is jailed for participating as an accomplice in a burglary that results in a murder. He keeps a diary of his experiences in prison and during the trial, alternating between regular diary entries and a screenplay script he is writing about his experiences. Though it is clear that Steve was asked to help with the burglary, it is unclear if he actually did so. There is great tension as Steve's prison experiences become more threatening and the trial winds to an uncertain conclusion. Josh liked the book because it is about a "boy like me" "who's in big trouble" and because some of "it's written like a movie".

Twice during our reading of the book, I had photocopied some pages onto half a sheet of paper and Josh had written a think-aloud, putting down what he was doing as a reader next to the text segments where he was doing it. From these think-alouds I knew that Josh was literally comprehending the story but that he was not making any kinds of inferences about the facts he was reading. Like many struggling readers, he understood the literal text but not the implied subtext. When he completed the novel, we had the following exchange:

Josh: There's one big thing I don't get. Did Steve Harmon take part in the robbery [that led to the murder] or not? I mean, it's bogus that he [the author] doesn't even tell us!

This comment confirmed for me that Josh needed my help to make some simple inferences. This was a slightly more sophisticated text than he was used to reading and it required him to infer by filling in gaps, and by seeing both simple implied relationships between details fairly close to each other and more complex implied relationships connecting and interpreting ideas from throughout various parts of the text. I knew that using additional think-alouds could help him to do these things.

➤➤ WHAT: First, I explained to Josh *what* he needed to do. I told him that expert readers go beyond the directly stated facts of a story and make inferences—they connect separate pieces of information, make guesses about missing scenes and data, and elaborate on story facts to make a more complete story. "You can answer your question about Steve by making some inferences. In fact, the author has laid out some clues for you and he expects you to pick up on these and make some inferences!"

➤➤ WHY: I explained to Josh *why* the strategy was important. "Most stories don't tell the whole story. You have to fill in gaps and read between the lines. The author gives you point A and point E and you have to walk to points B, C and D. If you don't make inferences then quite often you won't really understand the story."

➤➤ WHEN: Josh and I talked about *when* inferring is important in life, and in reading. I asked him how he could infer if I was in a good mood and why making such an inference might be important. We talked about times when he had only told someone part of a story and how he or she might infer the rest of what happened. I told Josh I would help him see where *Monster* invited him to make inferences: when there was a story gap, an unexplained connection, or an unanswered question. I asked, "Why do you sometimes leave certain things unsaid? Why might an author do this too?"

Josh smiled, "Like when I don't want my mom to know what I really did, or when I want someone to figure something out for himself."

I then asked Josh when he most believed Steve. "When he writes in his journal," he quickly answered.

"Most excellent!" I replied. "You are a reading prodigy, I can see already!"

Josh gave me a half smile, indicating that he thought I was hallucinating and that he didn't know what the word *prodigy* meant.

➤➤ HOW: I told Josh I would model *how* to infer as I thought aloud through my reading of the book's first few journal entries. In the first one, I got to this point in the diary entry. I read all the words of the story aloud and then inserted my thinking aloud as I did so (my thinking aloud is in bold).

TEXT	THINK-ALOUD
"You thinking about cutting a deal?" King asked.	**Geez, why would King threaten him? They're both on trial. They should be in this together.**
King curled his lip and narrowed his eyes.	**Yes, he is definitely threatening Steve! He is making a face at him to let him know he better not be making a deal and finking on him. But why would Steve need to cut a deal? Why would King be worried about him cutting a deal?**

 LENDING EXPERTISE: I was careful not to answer Josh's driving question. My interest wasn't in answering his question but in helping him learn a new process of reading that would help him in the future. My role was to point out where to look for information that might answer his questions and to model what to do with it—that is, to use the information to infer what the author wants us to understand about a character. With *Monster*, Walter Dean Myers is too good a writer to explicitly tell us that King is threatening Steve or why; he instead invites us to "fill in the gap" and infer an answer. Much as the pointillist painter Georges Seurat carefully placed thousands of small dots of color on a canvas, expecting us to use our mind's eye to fill in the gaps—to blend them to see a sunlit day in a Paris park—novelists invite us into a delightful process of reenvisioning their details and co-constructing their story with them so that we can experience it fully and make it our own.

 GUIDED PRACTICE: Later in the novel, I had Josh think aloud as he read a couple of diary entries, but I underlined key sections that required an inference. These underlines helped Josh become familiar with the kinds of moments in a text that signal a need for a reader to pose questions and infer. Kids need to know that fiction authors are in a sense continually extending different invitations to the reader: *come in, visualize this scene; caution, with these details about facial expressions and her tone of voice I'm telling you that she doesn't mean what she just said.* I was providing Josh with guided practice in noticing and interpreting such invitations to make inferences before I set him on his own. Here's an example:

TEXT	THINK-ALOUD
<u>Anybody can walk into a</u> <u>drugstore and look around.</u> <u>Is that what I'm on trial for?</u> <u>I didn't do nothing!</u>	**But Steve testified that he wasn't in the drug-store! So he was lying! Maybe he was trying to cover something up? But what he would be trying to cover up?**
<u>I thought about writing</u> <u>what happened in the drug-</u> <u>store, but I would rather not</u> <u>have it in my mind.</u>	**How could he write about it if he wasn't there? He must have been there! So he lied in the court. But why was he there? Did that mean he helped with the robbery? No wonder his lawyer doesn't believe him.**

 SCAFFOLDING: After several short think-aloud episodes where I underlined cues that were meant to stimulate inferences, Josh said that he thought he understood what inferring meant, could recognize when he was invited by authors to make inferences, and he also thought he had "kind of" an answer to his question: Steve was in the drugstore because he was supposed to help with the robbery but that it was left unclear whether he actually did help. "I think the author left it unclear on purpose," Josh told me, "to make us more involved… we're just like the jury then, judging him and trying to figure it out, if he's a monster or not. Personally, I think he decided not to help with the robbery and he was definitely out of there when the murder happened."

I talked with Josh then about how his evaluation of Steve's character led him to this conclusion and how that made him feel about the end of the book. Given Josh's enthusiasm for this story, and his growing ability to make inferences, I recommended that he read John Marsden's *Letters from the Inside.* "It's a mind-blowing book and it requires some major league inferring. Think you are up for it?" I asked Josh. He responded by borrowing the book and giving me a high-five. We discussed his reading of that book over several occasions, though in much less structured ways then we had worked through *Monster,* and it was clear that Josh was truly getting the hang of how to make inferences.

Inferring Is Crucial to Reading: Interpretive Strategies to Model for Kids

As I told Josh, quoting the great writer Umberto Eco, "Reading is the taking of inferential walks. The text offers point **A** and point **E**, and the reader must walk points **B**, **C**, and **D** to reach point **E**." Reading of all kinds requires continual inference-making, because so much of what an author communicates is not directly stated.

When working with a specific set of strategies, particularly complex ones such as inferring, I always find it useful to name for students the strategies we will use, the tip-offs in the text that remind us to use them, and how they will benefit us. Doing so makes very complex reading operations clearer and more accessible to students. It also "placeholds" the techniques and makes them more available as students go through their zone of proximal development to acquire and develop mastery. Following is an elaborated example of the kind of chart I devised with Josh and his classmates as we learned about inferring. (For more examples of guidance for using these kinds of "task-specific" reading processes, see Chapter 6).

Expert readers comprehend the literal text, make inferences based on textual details, and identify the clues upon which they have based their inferences by:

- noticing and comprehending literal details and building on these to predict future action and elaborate on the textual world
- noticing and filling textual gaps with relevant meaning
- noticing, connecting, and interpreting simple implied relationships (A reader must recognize a relationship that is not directly stated in the text. Readers must make an inference by connecting and interpreting a few pieces of information that occur close together in the text.)
- noticing, connecting, and interpreting complex implied relationships (Readers must infer a relationship and see a pattern from a large number of details that occur in

different places throughout a text. In order to answer such a question about a complex implied relationship a student must be able to "identify the necessary details, discern whatever patterns exist among them, and then draw the appropriate inference" (Hillocks 1980, 308)).

Expert readers do this so they can:

- make valid inferences about characters and their relationships
- make valid inferences about setting (the time and place)
- make valid inferences about past, present, and possible future action
- infer and identify the text-type and its expectations of the reader, i.e., recognize whether the text is nonfiction or fiction, realistic or fantasy, makes use of satire or irony, etc.
- infer and identify the mood and emotional tone of a text
- identify the point of view and attitude toward the material presented
- differentiate between the narrator and the author of a text
- infer the narrator's attitude toward the subject, others in the text, the reader
- judge the narrator's reliability (should we believe the narrator, and to what degree?)
- infer the author's attitude toward the subject and toward the audience
- use sets of inferences to figure out what an author is trying to communicate, i.e., the author's implicit meaning or "authorial generalization" about the subject matter (see page 131)
- elaborate and extend the text, applying it to future situations that go beyond the text itself.

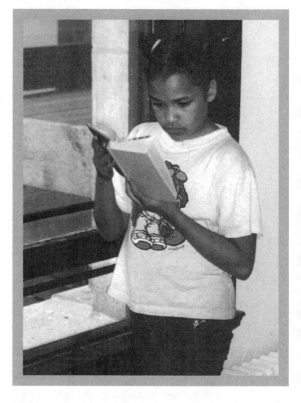

When students learn to infer, they can successfully engage and make meaning with texts that have a high inference load. Figuring out the puzzle of meaning keeps them from wanting to put the book down!

WHAT THINK-ALOUDS CAN DO FOR TEACHERS: OPENING THE WINDOW ON STRATEGIC INSTRUCTION

Our goal for students is engaged reading—that emotional and cognitive state when you are involved in a text to the fullest, using an author's words to get inside someone else's skin, understand another's point of view, connect this perspective to your own, converse with characters or an author, learn new information, and mysteriously come out with a changed understanding of yourself and your world.

Many of our students are not engaged readers and are not sure why the struggle to become one is worth it. More than that, they don't really know how to get started—they don't know what expert readers know and do when they read or how they might start doing these things too. It is our job to help them, and it's not a simple task.

In fact, when I work with preservice and practicing teachers, I often start my coaching by telling them, "You have a *big* problem. Well, you have at least one big problem that I know about!" The problem is that they (like you) are expert readers, and as such, they are unaware of all the cognitive, emotional, and visual processes they enact as they read. So automatic is their expert reading that it's hard for them to grasp the difficulties of those who most need their help, those who are least like them, the kids who are unmotivated to read and who don't do it very well. This makes it hard for us expert readers to teach these kids who don't understand why someone should want to read, much less to set about doing it in more productive ways. Think-alouds can provide immeasurable help. They make us slow down and take a look at our own reading process. They show us what students are doing—and not doing—as they engage in the reading process and they help students to take on our expert strategies.

Think-Alouds Can Help Teachers to...

- deepen their own awareness of the reading process
- use this heightened awareness of their strategic and interpretive processes to help model these strategies to kids
- see what students do and don't do as they read, which helps the teacher to assess

students and plan appropriate instruction in the students' "zone of proximal development"

- understand what in a text confuses readers; assess students' use of strategies; diagnose and address specific problems
- support readers to identify problems and monitor their own comprehension.

Think-Alouds Can Be Used to Model...

- general processes of reading, like predicting, monitoring and summarizing
- task-specific processes like understanding symbolism, irony, or bar graphs
- text-specific processes like understanding the structure of an argument and evaluating its effectiveness.

WAYS TO PRESENT THINK-ALOUDS

As you will see throughout this book, think-alouds can be introduced and used in a variety of ways, e.g., in spoken, written, or visual formats; on Post-it notes, overheads, butcher paper, or notebook paper.

Written think-alouds have the advantage of providing a record of reading activity that can be shared, manipulated, saved, assessed, compared to earlier and later efforts to gauge and demonstrate improvement, etc. These visible signs of accomplishment are very important to poorer readers. They can be used to celebrate improvement, put in a portfolio, and so forth. Basic ways to conduct think-alouds are:

- Teacher does think-aloud; students listen.
- Teacher does think-aloud; students help out.
- Students do think-alouds as large group; teacher and other students monitor and help.
- Students do think-alouds in small group; teacher and other students monitor and help.
- Individual student does think-aloud in forum; other students help.
- Students do think-alouds individually; compare with others.
- Teacher or students do think-alouds orally, in writing, on an overhead, with Post-it notes, or in journal.

STARTING POINTS

There are several strategies, called general reading processes, that researchers have discovered readers use every time they read anything. If your students don't do these things, this is the place to start your think-aloud modeling since these strategies will have the greatest pay-off for them across all reading tasks. The chart below defines these general processes.

General Processes of Reading

- Activate background/continue to personally connect to content throughout reading (activate and bring your appropriate background knowledge about reading and content to the reading task; use existing life knowledge to make sense of new information; apply what you are learning to your own questions and concerns).
- Decode text into words and meanings (occurs at word, sentence, and text levels).
- Set purpose for reading (think about whether you are reading for pleasure, for information, in order to converse with someone, in order to write, and so on, and read in an appropriate fashion to meeting your goals).
- Make predictions (create hypotheses and continually adjust them in light of new information).
- Visualize ("see" what you are reading; create a visual story world or mental model—with informational texts—that represents the meaning of the text).
- Ask questions (interrogate the text, the self, and the author before, during, and after reading).
- Summarize (bring meaning forward throughout the reading, determining what is important and continually synthesizing it with what has gone before).
- Monitor understanding/self-correct (continuously check that reading makes sense and use fix-it strategies when it doesn't).
- Reflect on meaning (consolidate knowledge with what was previously known).
- Prepare to apply what has been learned (create new knowledge structures, or schema, and ways of thinking and use these in new situations).

WHAT THINK-ALOUDS CAN DO FOR STUDENTS: OPENING THE WINDOW ON READING STRATEGIES

The power of think-alouds was revealed to me when I was researching for *You Gotta BE the Book* (Teachers College Press, 1997). Hoping to better understand what accounted for the difference between expert and at-risk adolescent readers, I designed a study to examine these two kinds of readers. I discovered that the expert readers continuously and simultaneously used *ten different dimensions* of interpretive strategies and response strategies during any particular reading of narratives (see box opposite). These strategies included general reading processes but went well beyond these to include many text- and task-specific processes particular to reading narrative. The kids who had intense difficulties with reading, on the other hand, couldn't identify or use a single interpretive response strategy. With this evidence before me, I asked: How can I help these poor readers? Where do I start? Knowing from the expert readers that *visualizing* and *participating in textual worlds* were two dimensions of response that were necessary to achieving response on other, more reflective dimensions, I chose these two strategies as a starting point. Using think-alouds, visual art, symbolic story representation, and drama, I helped the poorer readers to visualize while they read and to participate in a story world—to experience it as a character, for example. Once this basic level of response was achieved, the students were better able to use more reflective strategies, such as inferring and elaborating.

BOOK NOTES

For More on Engaged Reading

You Gotta BE the Book: Teaching Engaged and Reflective Reading with Adolescents (Wilhelm, 1997, Teachers College Press) lays out the theory of engagement and describes how expert adolescent readers engage with texts by making use of ten dimensions of response that include various meaning-making stances and strategies. The book also describes how unengaged readers can be helped to take on these expert stances and strategies through various instructional interventions such as drama and visual art.

Illuminating the Importance of Visualizing

Visualizing, I discovered, was perhaps the most obvious characteristic of student response to any kind of text, so much so that I've written that "Reading is Seeing" and that visualizing should be added to the general processes. I've also devoted a section to helping kids visualize through think-alouds in Chapter 5.

From these students, I noticed as well that readers of narrative have the particular challenge of visualizing characters, settings, and events. Students who did not intensely visualize and participate in "story worlds" did not engage with the text in other dimensions. In other words, if we don't help kids to visualize settings, characters, and action, then they will not be able to reflect on story action, the ways the story was constructed, what the story means, the author's purpose and perspective, and a lot of other things that expert readers of narrative do.

The point is that even reading a narrative has task-specific demands, as exhibited in the box below. (Reading informational texts also requires visualization, a kind—albeit a different kind—of a mental model.)

Interdependent Dimensions of Literary Response for Reading Narrative

ENTERING THE STORY WORLD
- Willingness to enter a story world.
- Entering the story world through interest in story action (and interest in character, setting, author, and other reasons).

IMAGINING THE STORY WORLD
- Seeing the story world: visualizing settings, situations, and characters.
- Relating to characters: becoming, empathizing with, and observing characters.

EXTENDING AND CONNECTING TO THE STORY WORLD
- Elaborating on the story world: noticing and inferring, embellishing and adding details, perhaps even creating new situations and episodes.
- Connecting: bringing and relating literature to one's life.

REFLECTING ON THE EXPERIENCED STORY WORLD
- Reflecting on the significance of events (theme) and behavior (judging characters).
- Noticing and reflecting on the constructedness of text, including the author's use of literary conventions, and why the author has constructed the text that way.
- Recognizing reading as a transaction; includes recognizing and conversing with author, her meaning, and her vision.
- Evaluating the author and the self as a reader; includes articulating understanding of one's own reading processes as part of that relationship.

Navigating New Text Structures

Sometimes educators and the public can get lulled into thinking that "reading is reading" and that if kids can decode words they can read any kind of text, no matter the text structure or conventions. This works as long as texts are familiar, simple, and fairly similar, but things quickly fall apart once students read different text types like ironic monologues, fables, satires, arguments or classifications, or texts that incorporate particular conventional tasks such as interpreting graphs, diagrams, symbolism, or irony for which they need to recognize these new text features and use new kinds of reading strategies. This is why teaching reading at the upper elementary levels and beyond requires a focus on text- and task-specific reading strategies.

Let's say that you drive a Toyota Camry with a stick shift. Your friend drives a Mazda. You ask to borrow her car. She tosses you her keys, you jump in, turn the ignition, and away you go, largely without thinking. How are you able to do this? The cars are so similar that driving one is much like driving the other. (My thanks to Michael Smith for this example.) Similarly, a fourth grader can move effortlessly from one R.L. Stine novel to another, because the task of reading this text is similar enough to the author's other novels; the reader can automatically transfer her skills to this new situation. Or a student who can easily read a narrative on a literal level will be able to move from one story to another and succeed in reading on a literal level again.

But now let's say your friend wants you to help her move, and you find yourself behind the wheel of a moving van with three clutches. Yikes! Now you slow down. You start talking to yourself. "First put the key in the ignition" you might whisper to yourself, "depress the first clutch and turn the key…." If something goes wrong, like the engine chokes out, you'll say, "Okay, let the clutch out a bit slower now…."

What's happened is that the task has changed. You can use some of the same skills you used from your previous driving experience, but you have to adapt those skills to a different situation and you have to develop some new skills too. If you've never driven a vehicle with a clutch, then you will need someone to model or talk you through the task, and you will certainly take the language and expertise she has lent you to talk yourself through your own first few repetitions of shifting gears.

When I asked Josh to move from a literal level of reading *Monster* to an inferential and interpretive one, it was like asking him to get out of the Mazda and get behind the wheel of that big moving van. Most texts that students read from fifth grade through high school require some level of inferring, connecting of inferences, judging of character, and main idea identification. Many of the reading skills they already possess need to be applied but some new skills also need to be awakened and exercised. Think-alouds help students take what they already know about reading and apply it to new reading situations. They also help students realize that in some cases they need to develop new skills for a text that makes new kinds of demands.

Assisting and Empowering Struggling Readers

In a research study I helped conduct concerning the literate activity of boys (Smith and Wilhelm, forthcoming), I was struck by how much all of the boys in the study expressed a desire for competence. They would go to great lengths to avoid tasks (like reading) that they did not feel they could competently complete. In classroom situations when think-alouds were provided that helped them to successfully complete, or at least successfully approach and improve, their performance on a difficult task, they were much more willing to undertake it.

Many of the boys felt reading was drudgery and that they weren't very good at it. Think-alouds allowed me and other teachers to model our own enjoyment and show reading as a pleasurable pursuit. Think-alouds also highlighted the problem-solving activity of readers, and showed kids that even teachers make mistakes and have to correct them. Many of the boys thought that expert readers never make mistakes (perhaps a function of the fact that we teach books we've read many times, as Rabinowitz and Smith, 1998, suggest) and that their own struggles showed how poor they were as readers. Having boys use think-alouds had the added benefit of revealing these students' unsuspected strengths. These were made apparent and I could name and celebrate them with the students. Many of the kids were later able to deduce and name their own strengths, weaknesses, areas of confusions, and progress by using their think-alouds.

Think-Alouds Help Students to:

- understand that reading should make sense! (Poor readers concentrate on decoding words and often do not make meaning or expect texts to make sense.)
- move beyond literal decoding to comprehending the global meanings of text. (Poor

readers have a limited, highly passive view of reading as simple decoding and acceptance of someone else's monolithic meaning. Expert readers understand that they do a lot of work with the text to responsively construct meaning and sense.)

- learn *how* to read by using many different strategies. (Poor readers have been shown to have a very impoverished idea of what reading really involves. They have a limited repertoire of strategies and may not be able to apply and use the strategies they possess in real reading contexts.)

- use particular strategies when reading particular text types. (National assessments show that many students master general strategies but do not understand that particular text-types or genres often require additional strategies.)

- share ways of reading. In sharing with peers and teachers, students see that reading is an enjoyable social pursuit through which they can relate to one another about texts and ideas. (Poor readers see reading as a private, solitary pursuit, rather than a social pursuit of conversing with authors, characters, and other readers. Much current research shows that teaching and learning are inherently social acts. Plus, Lev Vygotsky posited that two can often do together what neither can do alone. Reading together assists students.)

- learn about themselves and their own thinking and reading. This reflection helps students learn and use strategies on a self-conscious level. (This process is highly motivating, particularly for students disenfranchised by school, because their competence can be made evident by think-alouds. Poor readers are not aware of how they read and do not monitor and self-correct as they read. Expert readers are able to think about their thinking and reflect on their reading.)

ANSWERING THE BEDROCK QUESTIONS: WHY, HOW, AND WHAT WE SHOULD READ

All student readers need a motivating reason to read. This is particularly true of those reluctant readers who find reading hard work. If we want to help kids become better readers, we need to address three bedrock questions. Why should kids want to read particular texts? (What big and important purposes, both personally relevant and socially significant, can these texts play in their lives? How might reading these texts inform how they live, act, and make decisions?) A second consideration is how do expert readers read particular kinds of texts, and how can students be helped to read with the same genre-specific agility? (I address this throughout the book, particularly in Chapter 6.) The third consideration—and the only one, ironically, that ever receives much attention in schools—is: What should kids be reading? Personally, I think the answer to this last question depends almost entirely on the answers to the first two questions.

Why Read?

We read for lots of reasons, from profound to practical. We read to discover ourselves, for enjoyment, as a means to a college degree, to find a job, to find our way in an unfamiliar city. But whether we read to soothe our soul or program our VCR, it's fair to say that we read because we want to inquire about something important to us.

The research on reading and writing shows that these processes are best learned as forms of inquiry, and that they are best taught in the context of inquiry (Cf. Hillocks, 1995, 1999; Nystrand, 1997). What this means is that kids are most successful at learning new reading and writing strategies and on working through the new challenges posed by more difficult genres when they are reading and writing to do work and answer questions that are real and important to them.

For instance, the boys I've worked with through several studies typically didn't see any use for school reading (other than that it was part of "doing school"), and their motivation for such reading was low. They just didn't see a larger purpose for the reading they were required to do. On the other hand, both boys and girls in other situations were highly motivated to read when the reading was part of pursuing a compelling research question so they could enter into a larger debate or to make something that they cared about or that would demonstrate their learning.

Let's remember that kids have motivational zones of proximal development as well as cognitive ones. If we wish them to develop new interests, we must assist them by starting from the interests that they already possess.

I recently worked with both upper elementary and middle school students who were reading to answer big questions. One group of reluctant middle school boys asked the question: Who is the greatest baseball player who ever lived? They read with great gusto books about Babe Ruth and Mark McGwire, pored over statistics, read about the Negro Leagues (which none of them had ever heard of), and watched several documentaries, including Ken Burns's *Baseball*. They then made a video documentary of their own that argued that it was impossible to tell who the best ballplayer of all time is since so many great athletes were relegated to playing in the Negro Leagues instead of the majors, because of rule changes, and because of modifications to equipment and ball parks. Along the way, I was able to teach them many new strategies, including how to read arguments, evaluate data and warrants, make inferences and judgments, and make their own data-based arguments. They absorbed the strategies like sponges because they served their immediate interests and purposes. These boys were highly motivated and successful (many of their teachers were amazed at the amount of reading they did), because it was *their* question they were answering, not mine. As one boy put it, "We were interested, you know, and we were gonna make something about it to show what we learned and thought."

Though the techniques featured in this book will work with any text in various kinds of situations, it's my underlying assumption that all teaching of reading works best when students are inquiring into something of importance that they care about.

Literature has always been about inquiring into the human issues that are most significant, problematic, and meaningful in our lives. Informational texts obviously provide information on interesting and important topics that can be used to help us make decisions and do things. Kids inquiring about central life issues can use narrative, informational, and popular-culture texts (music videos, movies, song lyrics, comics, advertisements) to pursue their inquiries. When students read to inquire, it's easier to teach them processes of reading because they are motivated to read. As the teacher, you become someone giving them strategies that will help them to do their work. Collaborative, two-sided learning will be achieved.

What Should We Read?

A lot of time and energy is spent deciding what kids should read. I'd argue that before we make such a decision we should think about *why* kids might want to read about a topic or issue and negotiate it with them. I like to organize all the reading we do in my classes around research questions and "contact zones"—highly debatable issues to which no one really knows the answer. (Last year I had groups read about who was the greatest baseball player, whether music videos should be censored, if we should limit the lobster catch in Maine, the pros and cons of school uniforms, and many other similar topics.) I found that in every case I was able to include many of the important readings suggested by the curriculum, and all of the text-types suggested by the curriculum. Furthermore, I was able to meet all conceptual and procedural goals of the curriculum and the state test.

Once we've decided on a WHY and WHAT, then we can consider HOW (which is what the rest of this book will be about). Once we have a topic, then we can think about the kinds of texts we should read. We can consider the reading strategies the kids will need to be able to read these texts, and the activities that will give students practice with these strategies.

How Should We Read?

Through the rest of this book, I'll primarily use examples from a variety of units I've pursued with students from fourth through eighth grades, though I'll throw in an occasional high school example. Think-alouds work well with students of any age who are progressing to comprehend and interpret more challenging texts. I'll use lots of examples from students of different ages pursuing a thematic unit on love and relationships, which we organized around the question: What is a good relationship? This question is important to kids in the here and now, but it is also an important social question that will be important to their future happiness throughout their life. And it's easily integrated into the curriculum. Much of the literature that is typically used in schools (*Number the Stars, Bridge to Terabithia, Romeo and Juliet,* to name just a few) as well as popular-culture texts (cartoons, songs, movies) speak to this question.

Heading Down the River

I began and end this chapter with a learning story that takes place on a river in Maine.

Though I've enjoyed canoeing since I was a kid, I've just recently learned to white-water kayak. There are many canoeing skills that transfer, but there are many other task-specific expectations. I would have to adapt some of my previous skills to meet the demands of kayaking, and I would have to learn some new special skills. One of these would be the Eskimo roll, since white water kayakers often turn over and need to be righted quickly.

Unlike many of my reading students, I was already motivated to learn this new skill. I was eager to learn kayaking. I like outdoor sports and have lots of friends with whom I could pursue this sport. When we teach reading, it's helpful to make it something akin to kayaking: an adventure we will undertake together that will be challenging, requiring us to learn and use new strategies but that will be fun and will get us somewhere.

When I first got in a kayak, the teacher did not immediately send me through some rapids where I would have been sure to capsize. We worked for several sessions in a heated pool, learning how to get out of an overturned boat, how to "eddy out" of a river's current to get a rest, how to do a variety of strokes—some highly specific to kayaking—that are important on a river. All of these tools or strategies were explicitly taught in a situation that helped everyone in the class to be successful.

Nonetheless, I was surprised at how frustrated I became with learning the Eskimo roll. It was obvious to me and everyone else in the class that I could not get my kayak turned back over. I was the "remedial" student. Even though the class was highly supportive, the instruction appropriate, and my motivation high, I felt like quitting. I didn't understand why my competence as a canoeist was not translating to the kayak. The reason, of course, was the new task-specific expectations of the challenge. It occurred to me how much more difficult it is for our struggling readers who do not believe that reading can be fun, don't value it, and have behind them a lifetime of bailing out of their reading boats.

My teacher didn't give up on me. He arranged for an extra session, guided my paddle to the correct position as I hung upside down under the water, provided advice and language to "help you think and talk your way through it…. When you get turned over, set up, scratch your butt with the paddle end, look at your other paddle face, then kick your knee and roll your head toward your knee!" He had me recite these steps. He gave me some videotapes to watch of expert kayak rollers. Though I was far behind the rest of the class on rolling, one day I had a breakthrough! I hit four rolls in a row! Boy, was I excited! After a while, I was hitting 100 percent of my rolls in a pool. I had reached a new zone of actual development.

Then it was off to the river. This was a new zone of proximal development. The first few times that I turned over, I didn't even try to roll, I just got out of that dad-blamed boat as quickly as possible—I wasn't too happy with the rocks going by my head, the cold water, the lack of oxygen, and the roaring water.

Luckily my patient teacher was still supporting me. The next time we went to the river, he made me do several rolls in a quiet eddy on the river. I was successful. "Now," he said, "I want you to go into the current, roll over on purpose, and give it a try." This was a whole new set of demands and I had trouble. So we made adjustments. After a while I did a few successful rolls. I'll never forget successfully rolling over in heavy current, with water cascading out of my helmet, yelling, *"What's the problem? Because there is no problem!!!"*

Then he told me, "It will be harder still when you go over by surprise. At least make the attempt to roll. Just get it in your head that you won't bail out unless you've tried to roll twice!" (Think how powerful it would be if we could get our readers to try several self-correction strategies before they gave up on their reading! See Chapter 4 for more on that!)

I still don't hit all of my rolls, but I have confidence in myself and I get almost all of them. When I have a problem, I can talk my way to a solution. I have internalized much of my teacher's expertise and can use it to identify and solve problems.

Kayaking is a physical and cognitive skill that provides immediate feedback to the practitioner. If you aren't rolling your kayak it's pretty obvious. Reading is harder still. We need to be the kind of teacher that my kayak teacher is, constantly guiding and adapting instruction that is appropriate and contextualized. We need to recognize that being able to read one kind of text (or paddle one kind of boat) doesn't mean that you can read a different kind of text.

We need to remember that reading (even more so than kayaking!) is hard work, that teaching kids to read is hard work and will require constant attention, support, and adaptations. Even with good teaching, plan on small gains over time that will come in fits and starts. Though progress may seem slow and may even seem to regress at times, learning will be occurring, and one day you will find your students at the bottom of several rapids… or readings… that they can look back at and proudly say, "I read that!" Maybe they will even do some fist pumps and yell *"What is the problem?! Because there isn't one anymore!"* They will have learned something new, and they will be able to do that something on their own for the rest of their lives.

CHAPTER 2

WHAT ALL GOOD READERS DO:
Introducing General Reading Process Think-Alouds

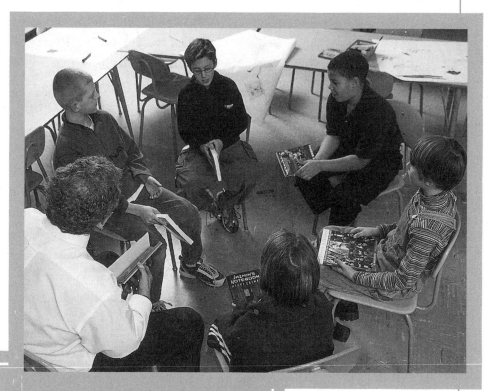

Fiona tells her reading group about the clues she used to make predictions during her reading. Her contribution is used to help compile a class list.

In the previous chapter, I listed the basic processes that all readers use every time they read. These are the general strategies—predicting, visualizing, and so on—that kids need to master before learning the task and text-specific processes I'll cover in later chapters. Because this set of general strategies is used with all texts, it is a good place to begin incorporating think-alouds into your teaching of literature and reading.

To show you how I plan and conduct a general-process think-aloud, and then follow it up with different kinds of think-aloud practice, let me introduce you to a bunch of sixth graders who chose to study the future of planet Earth. Their reasons for taking on this theme ranged from the altruistic:"I want to know how I can help make things like pollution and global warming better," to the practical, "Old people today don't know much about computers and other modern stuff, and I guess it's not their fault that they were born so long ago, but I want to think about my future…" to my pride-slashing favorite, "Mr. Wilhelm, I want to know what life will be like for me when I'm old like you!"

Okay, so with my delusions of remaining youthfully hip effectively banished, I decided to begin the unit with a shared reading of Gloria Skurzynski's *Virtual War*. I chose this novel because it is engaging and short. It paints a portrait of the fairly immediate future, which could shape our discussions. In the book everyone lives in domed cities due to nuclear fallout, and war for a few remaining safe havens is fought "virtually" over computers. The heroes of the story are teens who have been trained by electronic mentors since birth to engage in this virtual war. Though it's written for young adults, the book has a moderate inference load and deals with some heavy issues regarding personal freedom, genetic engineering, the environment, war, and violence.

Now I'll tease out the steps I took to plan and use think-alouds to teach some general-process strategies.

STEP 1: Choose a short section of text (or a short text).

Choose a text that is interesting to students, ideally with content that links to a current inquiry project. It ought to be challenging and present some difficulty to most of your students. Remember that Vygotsky said learning can only occur in the ZPD, so we want a text that students can read with your help, but that would give them significant difficulty on their own.

It works well to use the first page or two of a text with a think-aloud. Struggling readers tend to give up within the first few paragraphs; helping them to understand these passages gets them off to a strong start. And this helps orient all students to the kind of text it is, the vocabulary that will be used, and tips them off to the strategies they'll probably need to continue using. Of course, it's also great to work with a coherent piece of text, such as a short story (particularly if it's only a few pages) or a chapter (again, if not too lengthy).

Give each student a copy of the text. I usually introduce the first think-alouds by photocopying or typing the pages on the left-hand side of a sheet, and providing notebook lines on the right side on which they will write their responses to the text (see "The Chaser" example, page 73). Providing the lines reminds kids that I want them to respond moment by moment and line by line, and that their reading "moves" are in response to particular codes or writing "moves" that the author placed in the text.

Once students get the hang of it, they can simply put their notebooks next to their reading and record their responses there. If you can't do the typing or photocopying, put the text on transparency sheets and model your own think-aloud using the overhead projector.

STEP 2: Decide on a few strategies to highlight.

Explain to students how a think-aloud works and what strategies you will be trying out. Also brainstorm why and how these strategies will be helpful to them in their own reading.

With *Virtual War,* I primarily spotlighted one strategy: predicting and correcting predictions. I focused particularly on predicting future action and making predictions about characters: what they were like and what they would do. (Making character predictions merges with inferring character, which might be considered a more text-specific strategy of reading narratives, but I focus on it here as a more general strategy of predicting). I felt that the kids were ready to consider how authors construct stories to lead us on, create interest and suspense. Since our unit was about the future, the whole notion of making predictions and adjusting our behavior to discourage or encourage our predictions to come true seemed very central to our study. The students were also ready to consider how authors create character, and the concept of character is heightened in this novel; the teens' characters are shaped by genetic mutation and rearing by computer programs.

To summarize, I decided to focus on prediction because I felt it was in the students' zone of proximal development, because it was necessary to our unit of study, and because the plot of this text, like our unit, is in a sense one big prediction about what life will be like in the not-so-distant future. I knew that during the unit we would try to surmise various authors' predictions about the future and converse with them about these, which is another important reading skill and a springboard that can lead us to more future reading and inquiry.

What the Research Says

Studies of teaching generally show that trying to do more than three things at once distracts student attention from all of the elements. *It's better to focus and really address a few goals rather than diffusing energy by trying to address too many.* Kids can easily be overwhelmed by "sensory overload!" as one of my middle school students likes to say. Start where the students are and focus on one or two new strategies that they are ready to learn and use. Once students are familiar with think-alouds and have mastered the highlighted strategies, then you can cast a wider net and progress to a focus on more sophisticated strategies, one or two at a time.

STEP 3: State your purposes.

In this case, I would tell students that the purposes of reading *Virtual War* are to:

- enjoy a really good story about kids in the future who are just a bit older than they are;

- get us started on our agreed upon inquiry into the future (these first two goals pertain to setting purposes for reading, a general-process strategy that I won't be emphasizing with the kids now);

- learn some strategies that will help us in our inquiry, namely, making and adjusting predictions, and understanding how character is formed both in the real world and in the story world the author has created, so that we can enter into characters' experiences and predict what they might do and feel.

Tell students that as you are thinking aloud, you want them to pay attention to the strategies you use so they can explain what, why, how, and when you used them. This is wonderful for sharpening their attention!

STEP 4: Read the text aloud to students and think-aloud as you do so.

I read the text slowly and stop quite often to report out, doing my best to target the focus strategies of predicting and inferring character, though other general strategies like asking questions naturally kick in too.

When a teacher says aloud—reports out—all he is noticing and doing as he reads, students finally "see" all the steps and motions of an expert reader.

When I report out during the first few think-alouds, I put the text down, look at students, and say "Hmmm…" to signal that I am shifting from reading to thinking aloud.

First, I preview the book, wondering aloud about the title, the cover illustrations, the back cover, and so on.

Hmmm. I predict this book will be about a war fought on computers, like a computer game.

[Looking at cover illustration] ***Hmmm. I see three people, but their heads don't fit their bodies and they are on a computer screen with computer code. I bet these are the people who will fight the virtual war, or maybe they are knowbots who will fight the war on-screen. I predict that they are really smart and that is why their heads are so big. One of them looks younger than the others and mutated or something. They all have boxes around their necks… I bet that's important but I don't know why.***

The sky was golden.	**Hmmm. I know the first lines of text are important and I should notice them. This one's funny—skies aren't usually gold. I wonder if this means he's happy, or it's a great day or something.**
Corgan could feel sand beneath his fingers. What were those trees called, he wondered, the tall ones that curved to the sky…	**Hmmm. I predict he means palm trees. But why doesn't he know the name? He doesn't sound very well informed. I wonder why not? I predict that he is trained to know about only certain things. But the first thing he does in this book is ask a question. I bet he has an inquiring mind.**
What does it matter, he thought. Things don't need names. They haven't told me the names of lots of things, and I don't really care. It's nice to lie here like this under the sky and the trees and not have to practice for a while.	**Hmmm. Who are these "they"? They must be people who teach or control Corgan. These "they" must make him practice all the time… I bet they are making him practice to fight the virtual war. He seems to accept the way things are since he says "I don't really care." Or maybe he does care but he can't do anything about it. I'll have to read further to find out. I wonder if it will be like the movie *The Matrix?* I think it's weird that he doesn't know the names of things. I wonder why "they" are withholding information from him.**
A girl walked across the beach… and his LiteSuit began to shimmer with the color of blood.	**Hmm. I wonder if that's because she's beautiful. I predict that the LiteSuit reflects his mood or feelings because if his LiteSuit turns red and shimmers I bet that means he is excited or interested by her. Things shimmer when they are excited or stimulated.**

TEXT	THINK-ALOUD
Corgan knew what blood looked like. Once, a few months ago, as he'd walked along the tunnel from his Box to his Clean Room, a tile fell from the ceiling and hit his hand. His knuckles had bled, the first and only time he had ever seen real blood.	**Hmmm. There sure is a lot on this first page! This is weird. Why has he only seen blood once? I predict that he must be totally protected... I bet that he is special in some way; I can't imagine that they would spend that much attention on everybody, plus he must be one of the main characters of this book.**
The way the Supreme Council had carried on it was as if Corgan's arm had been chopped off or something.	**Hmmm. Who is the Supreme Council? The "they"? I don't know. I predict that they might be the people playing at the Virtual War. I predict that they are certainly the people who are controlling Corgan. I predict that there must be a lot of contamination and sickness if they worry about a little cut. Corgan must be really special in some way and being protected, probably to fight the Virtual War. I'll bet that's it.**

I continue thinking aloud for another page before cycling on to the next step. Notice that I *name* certain text features (title, illustration, the importance of the first few lines of text), and explain why I'm looking especially closely at them to help me make sense of things. As you report out, demonstrate the way expert readers notice text features and interpret these (see Rules of Notice, pages 77–80). Use verbs like, I *wonder*, I *think*, I *predict*, I *bet*, I'm *confused* to spotlight the kinds of mental moves you are making. Use phrases like *I'm going to reread*, or *I'll have to read further*, or *I don't know* to both highlight reading strategies and show kids that as an expert reader stitches together an understanding of a new text, it's okay that he has some loose threads—it's okay that he doesn't know, that he is going to have to read on to find out. That's what predictions are—best guesses that we suspend in our heads, that the text will either prove were on target or in need of correction.

STEP 5: Have students underline the words and phrases that helped you use a strategy.

For example, after completing my think-aloud of the first two pages of *Virtual War*, I have my students underline the phrases that they think helped me infer about character (primarily Corgan) and make predictions about his situation. We then talk about exactly how Gloria Skurzynski—and by extension, other authors—introduce characters and begin painting a portrait of their personalities. We also talk about foreshadowing, how authors lay hints about future action so that we can predict and anticipate what may happen next, feel suspense, and perhaps be tricked.

As I continue to read aloud, the students underline clues to future action: they underline details about the Go-Ball match with the beautiful girl Sharla, and predict that it was a test for the Virtual War; they underline a description of how Corgan was distracted by Sharla and predict that the enemy in the Virtual War will also try to distract him. When Mendor, Corgan's teacher, enters the scene, the students are able to confirm these predictions and learn that the Virtual War is only 17 days away and that Corgan will be the one to fight it.

I like to have students make predictions and underline the clues that led to their predictions. After reading a section, students can go back and see whether their predictions were borne out, proven wrong, or remain inconclusive. Stephanie Harvey (2000) suggests that students go back after reading to code their predictions with A+ if it came true, A− if it did not and an "0" if the evidence is inconclusive.

STEP 6: List the cues and strategies used.

After I have done some thinking aloud with students using a particular strategy, I ask them to make a list of the signals that prompt us to use the strategy. Authors create character, for example, through details about a character's looks, diction, thoughts, clothing, actions, friends, comments from others, favorite surroundings, and so on. They expect us to piece together these cues to infer character. I then ask students which cues they used or underlined and which they did not. Then I ask them to continue using the cues they did and to make a renewed effort to attend to cues they did not use yet.

I like to keep the lists of such cues on the classroom wall.

STEP 7: Ask students to identify other situations (real world and reading situations) in which they could use these same strategies.

Research on reflection (e.g. Edmiston, 1992) shows that asking students in the midst of an activity (or immediately after) what strategies they are using and how they could be used in other situations helps students learn and transfer these strategies to other contexts.

General-process strategies all are used in particular ways during reading, but they also mirror parallel operations in real life. For instance, we often must summarize activity, monitor how we are doing, make predictions, or infer character. In order to connect the strategy to my students' lived experience I will segue from predictions to the topic of the future that we are studying. Why do we need to predict things about the future? How does that help us? Who tries to predict the future and how do they try to do it? How do people try to predict or plan their own personal futures? Why is that important? How well do different prediction strategies work? What evidence are such predictions based on?

Progressing to characterization, I might now ask my sixth graders such questions as: How do you decide what a person is like? How do you determine if you like a person when you first meet him? And, Why are first impressions so important? What are some things you notice as you interpret first impressions? Or I'll ask them about me—what they've noticed, and why it's important to figure out what I'm like.

Then they can brainstorm other textual and real life situations, as well as people it's important to figure out and make predictions about.

Consider This

<u>Before linking</u> the think-aloud process to reading, you may wish
to have students think aloud with something more concrete and accessible to
them. Have them do a think-aloud for a physical task with which they are familiar.
The possibilities are endless: I've had kids do this for splitting wood, fly casting,
programming a VCR, turning on e-mail, carving a ski turn, cooking spaghetti, even
for making a peanut butter sandwich.

- Tell them that the think-aloud is for someone who doesn't know how to do
  the activity. I ask them to tape-record the think-aloud as they actually
  engage in the process. Kids could also write it out, of course.

- Ask them to first state the purpose of the activity, then describe how they
  prepare and get started. Then they can record everything that they think,
  notice, and do as they engage in the activity, as well as how they reflect on
  and evaluate their performance.

- Afterward, ask the class to discuss what we can learn about an activity by
  doing a think-aloud as we engage in it versus what we learn by listening to
  someone else talk through a task.

STEP 8: Reinforce the think-aloud with follow-up lessons.

The "eighth step"—and it's a crucial one—is to extend and consolidate the strategies
introduced in the initial think-aloud. A new strategy requires guidance and practice to
internalize. You can provide this both by using the same text to do more think-alouds
with the strategy, or with a new text. Following are a few teaching techniques my colleagues and I have had success with. You'll only use some of these activities some of the
time, but you will want to have all these tools in your tool kit. *And they work well with
any of the types of think-alouds discussed in this book.* I've organized them generally along
the Vygotskian teaching continuum so you will get a sense of how you might use them
to gradually remove the scaffolded assistance and release responsiblity for the strategy use

to the student, but most of the techniques could be adapted to fit on various points of that continuum.

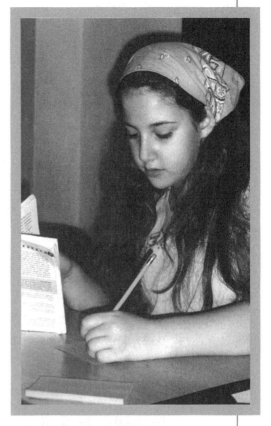

A student writes down her think-aloud on a Post-it note.

TEACHER DOES/STUDENT WATCHES

MODELING—AND MORE MODELING

Do lots of teacher-modeled think-alouds, particularly of new strategies. Use real texts of immediate interest so that modeling is always done in the context of meaningful reading. Then gradually release responsibility over to the students. Remember the fishing practice of "catch and release"—students should catch the new strategy, or the full repertoire of strategies needed to approach a text, before you release them to angle the text on their own.

TEACHER DOES/STUDENTS HELP

THINK-ALONGS

As you read aloud and think aloud, students follow along. A good way to introduce this is to have *students* identify and say aloud the kinds of moves and strategies you report on, and explain why these are useful and important. They literally "think along" with you and articulate what it is you are doing and why, immediately after you report on a particular move. As they improve they can identify the prompts that show a particular move should be made.

For example, I was recently reading *Pobby and Dingan* with fourth graders. This is a wonderfully written and offbeat young adult book out of Australia. (It does contain some strong language, but the students I was working with absolutely loved it.) It's about the reality of two imaginary friends and what happens to a family, particularly a callow older brother, when his younger sister's two imaginary friends go missing in an opal mine because of the family's carelessness.

As I read the first passage about how Kellyanne's imaginary friends Pobby and Dingan are "maybe-dead," I thought aloud, "I wonder what has happened to them? I bet this story is starting here and will flash back to explain what has happened to

Pobby and Dingan. I'll bet something bad has happened to Kellyanne and that has made her feel like her imaginary friends have left her." My fourth graders immediately identified my moves as "wonderings" or "lots of predictions." I then told them my first prediction was one about story construction as I guessed that this story was starting in the middle of something, and my other prediction concerned story content— about what actually would happen in the story. When I asked the kids why I had made this move, one fourth grader said, "The author is starting in the middle because he wants us to wonder what happened. And we know it must be something bad for them to be 'maybe-dead,' so we make predictions and it makes us want to read more to find out if we are right!"

 ## Teacher Does/Students Do

Strategies Lists

Together with students, create a list of the strategies you're using and post it on the board as a reference for students. Students can use this list to guide their own strategy use, to identify strategies they are using, to identify strategies that weren't used but could have been, and so forth. Sometimes students will make an effort to come up with a new strategy to add to the list.

Posting these lists around the classroom can serve as a reminder to students of what things they are supposed to do when they read. Students can build from these lists to devise symbols for various strategies to facilitate self-assessment. They can then code others' or their own think-alouds to see what strategies they are using and not using (for more information about this kind of coding, see pages 171–172 in Chapter 7).

Based on our discussions of my think-alouds, we created a class list of foreshadowing clues (e.g., "story starts in middle—have to figure out what happened before!" "there is a problem—how will it get fixed?"), prediction moves ("wonder what happened before" "guess what will happen next" "figure out what the story is really about"), and reasons to predict ("makes you want to read and find out what happens" "helps you think about what is happening" "makes suspense!" "like a game—see if you are right!").

We talked about why predictions were such an important move at the beginning of a text, and then proceeded to think about other moves I had made in my think-alouds over the first few pages of *Pobby and Dingan*. Our list was then expanded to look like this:

wonder about what happened before

predict what will happen next

figure out who characters are and what they are like (by reading inner thoughts, expressions, feelings, how they look, what they say, etc.)

figure out why characters are doing what they are doing (especially why Kellyanne has imaginary friends!) (study behaviors and figure out probable motives)

see the house in your mind (pretty weird, with car doors between rooms!), and the town and the opal mine. (look for details about the setting, visualize it in your mind, and figure out what it would be like to be there)

TEACHER DOES/STUDENTS DO

READ ALOUD/PAUSE/WRITE

As you think-aloud, pause at certain points, have students write down what they are thinking and doing at that point in the text, and then all take turns sharing your moves. For example, in Chapter 2, Kellyanne's dad takes Pobby and Dingan to his opal mine and promises to take good care of them. I paused, and the students and I all wrote down what we were thinking. Most of them correctly predicted that dad would lose Pobby and Dingan and upset Kellyanne. For those who did not make this prediction we noted the clues the successful predictors had used, for example that dad had gone overboard assuring Kellyanne that her imaginary friends would be fine, and because dad appeared to have forgotten about them when he arrived back home.

With this activity, students can compare their strategies to yours and to those of their peers. They will discover that there are many ways to get meaning from a text and that every reading is unique. They will learn that some strategies and readings are not as appropriate and rich as others—but perhaps more importantly, they will borrow and adapt strategies to suit their needs.

TEACHER DOES/STUDENTS DO

TALK-THROUGHS

With this one, students "talk through" their reading response as I read a section of text aloud. This provides great "scaffolding" in preparation for when I will ask them to read *and* talk through/write down their own reading activity. It's simpler for them because I am doing the reading, so they are freer to concentrate on responding to the piece. I usually read, pause, and ask students to write down their responses to the passage I have read, and then have just one or two students read aloud what they wrote. At other times, I'll ask all students to jump in with their thinking as soon as I'm done reading a passage. Perhaps we'll go around the class, or perhaps we will play "Just Jump In," for which every student knows they have to take two turns sometime during the activity. (Sometimes I ask kids to stand and they are allowed to sit once they have made a contribution. I also sometimes give kids two objects which they deposit in a basket when they contribute. They know that they have to get rid of both objects during the think-aloud.)

Once students understand the gist of how think-alouds work through such shared activities, I then ask them to read and do their think-aloud responses on their own.

STUDENTS DO/TEACHER HELPS

RESPONSE FORUM

With a forum (also known as a fishbowl), I start a think-aloud and then ask a student volunteer to "take the stage" by taking over the think-aloud for a short period. I might take over again for a while before asking for another volunteer, depending on whether there is something I want to model. The student who takes the stage is usually at the front or middle of the classroom, where she can be observed by the forum—the class or small group. (I prefer working in groups of four to six students but it can be done as a whole-class activity.)

When a think-aloud segment is over, other students may jump in to comment. To give these comments from the forum some structure, I like to use the PQP format:

- first some Praise
- then some Questions
- then some Polish suggestions—corrections, additions, and the like

Or use the LaW and Order format:

- First give L comments—something you Liked about the think-aloud, or something you learned from it.
- Then W comments—something you Wondered about the think-aloud.
- Then O comments—friendly "Orders" you'd like to have the reader try, suggestions you might have for them the next time they do a think-aloud.

I think these kinds of prompts and guidelines help all students to voice a response and encourage them to make comments that are productive, varied, and that help the class celebrate a text as well as set goals for future reading challenges. Otherwise, I often find that my students do not make constructive comments and that they particularly avoid providing suggestions for improvement. To reinforce the importance of helping each other, I sometimes conclude my lessons by having students ask each other: "I wonder what would happen if you... [tried to do/use a particular strategy]" as a gentle way of making a suggestion.

At other times, though, you'll want the forum to "just jump in" to report out on the passage, so they can bounce their ideas off the student who's onstage. As we work through a text in this manner we create a "group mosaic" or group think-aloud of various people's responses. This is a dynamic way to begin turning over the task to students. Your presence and the collaborative nature of this work provide a safety net that helps guide students to ever more independent performance.

 ## STUDENTS DO/TEACHER WATCHES AND ASSESSES

THOUGHT BUBBLES

Some students take to think-alouds immediately, instantly knowing what you mean when you describe thinking about thinking or thinking about reading. They may already be using the strategies you highlight, even if they haven't named them or manipulated them. Other students don't have any experience with metacognition, and may not have ever used the strategies you are spotlighting. Such students may be less willing to think out loud. For these students, "thought bubbles" are just the ticket.

I draw a picture of a reader with a thought bubble above his or her head. For fun, students might even draw their own picture, paste a school picture of themselves on the face, and so forth. I'll make several copies of each picture so that students can use them to record several think-aloud moves. Then I ask them to write something they are thinking into the thought bubbles at various points in the text. When a thought bubble is filled, or when they move on to a different section of text, they then use a new thought bubble.

For example, at the end of Chapter 2 of *Pobby and Dingan,* the father has been arrested for "ratting" or trespassing on another miner's opal claim while he was looking for the missing imaginary friends. Kellyanne's brother Ashmol ends the chapter by thinking "of Dad and if he was in prison and how the whole thing was Pobby and Dingan's fault. And then I tried to get my head round how it could be their fault if they didn't even exist."

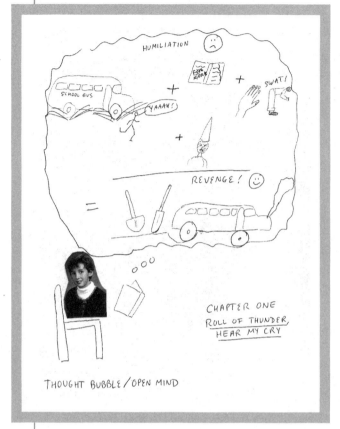

HUMILIATION

SCHOOL BUS

YAAAW!

+

+

SWAT!

+

REVENGE! :)

=

CHAPTER ONE
ROLL OF THUNDER,
HEAR MY CRY

THOUGHT BUBBLE / OPEN MIND

Fiona creates a thought bubble of her response to the Logan children's revenge on the school bus in the book *Roll of Thunder, Hear My Cry* and the various factors that contributed to their desire for revenge.

Jazzy, who had not spoken yet during the class, filled out her thought bubble by writing: "They are real because people act like they are real. And that is how it is everybody's fault." Jazzy was then asked to explain her comments and how this judging of characters was helping her as she read.

Completing several—say five to ten— thought bubbles usually successfully ushers more reluctant readers into using think-alouds more independently. It's also a great transition to the techniques of visual think-alouds, described in Chapter 5.

 ### STUDENTS DO/TEACHER WATCHES AND ASSESSES

OPEN MIND

With this extension, pairs of students complete the think-aloud begun as a whole group (or begin a new one with a new text), with one person reading aloud and pausing, the other reporting out. Then students switch roles. The benefit? Students support each other, and can then widen their repertoire of strategy use by sharing their work with another pair or the larger group.

I encourage students to get started by

Two students conducting "open mind."

"opening their mind." If they have trouble, I tell them to just say whatever is happening in their mind. Even if they say "This is boring!" or "I don't know what to do," this is a start, and gives you valuable information about their level of awareness and response to the reading. You may learn that you have to do more work to get them engaged in the content of the text, or help them to use a strategy of some kind to get started. If they truly do not understand the strategy or its use, it is important to get this kind of feedback so that you can intervene.

▶▶ STUDENTS DO/TEACHER WATCHES AND ASSESSES

FLAG THE TEXT

Using Post-it notes as a tool for comprehension monitoring is common. I first learned about this nearly twenty years ago in the National Writing Project, and have had many students, like Kelly Chandler, "The queen of Post-its," who have used these sticky pieces of paper in many creative ways.

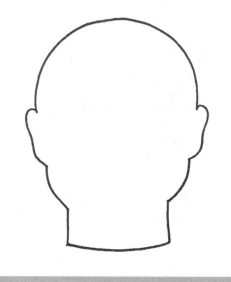

VISUAL OPEN MIND

[Reproduce this graphic for your students to complete]

Students can draw or write in their thoughts while reading a particular passage. The picture could be divided into sections prompting particular kinds of strategies, questions, etc.

Post-its can be very useful with think-alouds. For example, if students are reading a textbook that they can't write in, they can always record their thoughts on Post-its, sticking them right on the text as they respond.

Or, it works very well to have small groups of students read the same story and then pool their Post-its onto one copy. If I give each student *different-colored* Post-its, they can see the similarities and differences in the number and types of strategies group members used. Sometimes I ask students to use particular colors for a particular strategy use, for instance one color for predictions, another for personal connections, and a third for visualizations. In this way, students can see at a glance how often they use each strategy and how the strategies are integrated throughout a story.

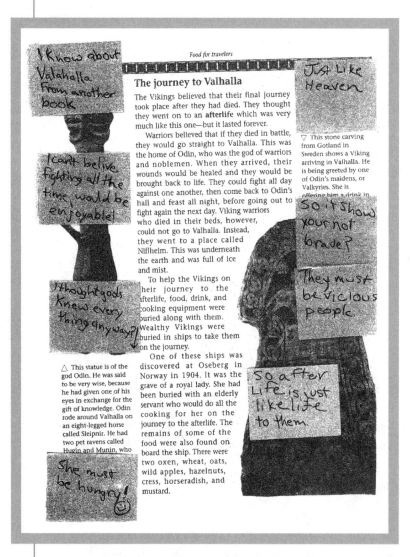

Food for travelers

The journey to Valhalla

The Vikings believed that their final journey took place after they had died. They thought they went on to an **afterlife** which was very much like this one—but it lasted forever.

Warriors believed that if they died in battle, they would go straight to Valhalla. This was the home of Odin, who was the god of warriors and noblemen. When they arrived, their wounds would be healed and they would be brought back to life. They could fight all day against one another, then come back to Odin's hall and feast all night, before going out to fight again the next day. Viking warriors who died in their beds, however, could not go to Valhalla. Instead, they went to a place called Niflheim. This was underneath the earth and was full of ice and mist.

To help the Vikings on their journey to the afterlife, food, drink, and cooking equipment were buried along with them. Wealthy Vikings were buried in ships to take them on the journey.

One of these ships was discovered at Oseberg in Norway in 1904. It was the grave of a royal lady. She had been buried with an elderly servant who would do all the cooking for her on the journey to the afterlife. The remains of some of the food were also found on board the ship. There were two oxen, wheat, oats, wild apples, hazelnuts, cress, horseradish, and mustard.

△ This statue is of the god Odin. He was said to be very wise, because he had given one of his eyes in exchange for the gift of knowledge. Odin rode around Valhalla on an eight-legged horse called Sleipnir. He had two pet ravens called Hugin and Munin, who

▽ This stone carving from Gotland in Sweden shows a Viking arriving in Valhalla. He is being greeted by one of Odin's maidens, or Valkyries. She is offering him a drink in

Handwritten Post-it notes:
- I know about Valhalla from another book
- I cant belive fighting all the time would be enjoyable!
- I thought gods knew everything anyway?
- She must be hungry!
- Just Like Heaven
- So it show your not brave?
- They must be vicious people.
- So after Life is just like life to them.

Those think-aloud Post-its show a student asking questions and making personal connections, judgments, and comments in the service of understanding this text.

When you're finished reading a story, students can collect the Post-its in order and create a **response timeline** of their reading of a text. I usually have them do this on a roll of butcher paper that we hang in the classroom. Sometimes I post the pages of a story in order, spacing them a foot or so apart. Students attach their response around the appropriate page, perhaps drawing a line from their Post-it to the words or phrases that stimulated that response. At other times I might just write the major events or details on the bottom of the butcher paper and let the students attach their Post-its above the events or details they responded to. There are obviously various ways to do this.

As a great way to have kids self-assess their strategy use, have them collect and classify Post-its of one or several texts they've read. For example, when Jazzy collected her thought bubbles halfway through our reading of *Pobby and Dingan,* she noticed that she had only eight Post-its (which was relatively few) and almost all of her comments were judgments about character. "I'm always telling them they are wrong or making a

Improving Comprehension with Think-Aloud Strategies • Scholastic Professional Books

mistake or something. Or sometimes I am trying to make them feel better like Kellyanne." After we had celebrated what a useful strategy this is (trying to be a help-mate for a character), I asked Jazzy if there were other strategies she could try to use more often. "I think I could make more predictions about what they might do once they figure out their mistakes," she told me.

Like any other think-aloud record, students' Post-it responses become valuable resources for when they write about a piece of literature or their reading process. In the example below, Phil uses this raw material to write an analysis. I added comments to highlight the richness of his response.

Written Analyses of Reading <u>Heart of a Champion</u> and <u>With the Vikings</u> by Phil (5th grade)

I was reading <u>Nighthoops</u> and some other Carl Deuker books and I liked it because I like basketball and it wasn't like most books that are boring and where not too much happens. <u>Nighthoops</u> had lots of action and it wasn't all about basketball. It was about making friends with a guy who was wild and needed help but it was all related to the basketball. It all had a relationship to the game. I liked that, that everything hung together, so I thought I would read another one.

> **understands action and subtext**

> **Think Aloud prompt** Personal connection: expression of interest

When I started reading <u>Heart of a Champion</u>, the first thing I noticed was that his dad had died. I kind of wondered what that would have to do with the book. Then I read that his dad was a golfer and wanted Seth to golf too, and Seth would do whatever other people wanted him to do. That really bugged me. And with his dad gone, he could do more of what he wanted, and this was how he got into base-ball. And I was kind of mad about that, that he couldn't make his own decisions and all that.

> **think aloud practice taught Phil that it's good to engage emotionally with text**

But then this doing what other people wanted kept getting him in trouble. I noticed that this was like the major thing in the book. Like this older kid wanted him to drink, and Seth just took it, but his friend wouldn't do it so then Seth wouldn't do it either and I thought why can't you just make up your own mind?

> **notices repetition and relationship to theme**

> **judges character**

And later on he started drinking because there is always pres-sure, isn't there? At the end of the book his friend Jimmy died from drinking and driving. And they dedicated the next game to Jimmy and they won. But then they lost the next game. That surprised me and I put a big exclamation mark on my think-aloud post it. Then I was thinking that the author was showing that if you have a big life problem you can't just solve it and la la la everything gets fixed. You have to really work hard to stay out of trouble and to get out of trouble once you are in it.

notices surprise— how his expectations weren't met and what this means

After I thought about it I liked how the season ended so quick and unexpected, just like Jimmy dying, when they thought things would keep on going. All through the book, good things followed the bad things, except at the end. I think that showed how some mistakes are so big that you can't fix them, you just have to live with them.

evaluates constructedness of text and relationship to story meaning

So how did I read this? I read it being totally in to the story and the baseball, but I really started caring and following the characters, and judging them. Then later on I started thinking about the author and why the author did things the way he did, especially when he started surprising me towards the end and things didn't turn out how I thought. I was sad at the end, almost a little disappointed. Jimmy was a great guy but he ruined his life. What a waste, and he hadn't even learned from his dad's mistakes because his dad was an alcoholic. I just thought of this. The game tied his life together. He always did his best in games. But he wouldn't do his best in life. Why not? He could get up for the game but not for life? So he was a champion in the game but not in life. I guess that's what I like about these books, they wrap everything together.

expresses a relationship to and evaluation of author

his think-aloud and his writing help him achieve a sense of coherence

With the Vikings

I read this different than I read the Heart of a Champion. I didn't find it half as interesting. It wasn't about something I like to do or that I like. I mean it was so old. It had nothing to do with me. I guess I want what I read to be about me and my life. I mean I had a choice but it had to be about history and history is history.

Phil shows an awareness that books of different genres require different stances (see chapter 6) and strategies

assesses self as a reader

I basically was reading the other book [Heart of a Champion] for enjoyment and for the story. This I was reading for information which I automatically think of as boring. I had to write this picture book for my reading buddy so I had to find stuff that would be interesting to her. So I took notes. Whenever I found something sort of interesting, I would

cites strategy for remembering and placeholding important information make a note so I would remember. When I was done I felt relieved. Like I felt, good, that's done, now I can write the book. It was like this was something I had to do to do something else. The other book the point was reading. Here the point was researching and learning and then writing. I like writing, but here it was the topic that bugged me. I liked making the book though, that was cool. Especially the pictures and the pictures in the books I read really helped with that, to get the pictures right.

In fact, my students, like all adolescents, enjoy perusing these artifacts of their thinking, or more to the point, *love* this kind of self-analysis! (One student informed me "To know me is to love me!" I asked him why he was so sure. His reply: "I know myself really well and I really love myself.")

PROMPTS THAT GUIDE STUDENTS TO USE THE GENERAL READING STRATEGIES

As you create your own lessons, use the following list of strategies/prompts as a checklist of general process strategies to teach and how to teach them. Use the six steps of recursive instruction (page 13) to guide students toward independence with them. For more on how to help students monitor their use of the strategies, turn to Chapter 7.

First, some management tips:

- You could go through the strategies in the order presented, but you don't have to. And you don't have to go through *all* the strategies; you should focus on what you think your students most need.

- When I introduce these general processes to my students, I do it by *introducing a couple at a time with short texts.* We put the strategies and prompts on chart paper and post them with illustrations at the front of the classroom.

1. Set Purposes for Reading

There is a host of research that shows how vitally important it is to model purpose-setting for kids. When students don't have a personal purpose for reading, they have problems identifying key details—not to mention difficulty staying engaged. In fact, students generally don't see a purpose for school reading. It's up to us to have a compelling rationale—and name it for students—with every book we read. (I'm indebted here to the work of Bauman, 1993; and Davey, 1983 who provide the basis for some of the prompts that follow.)

Start by talking through how you naturally preview a text. Use the following prompts.

BOOK SELECTION/PREVIEWING PROMPTS

Sample Prompts that Relate to Considering a Book's Content, Genre, Readability

"The title/author/call-outs/pictures/front matter/author information/book design/text this is in/makes me think…"

"The title makes me think that this is going to be about a car race."

"The book this is in makes me think that this is going to be about science in everyday life, probably about electricity."

"The photographs make me think that this will be about really bad storms."

"The comments on the back make me think that professional football players think this book really captures the life of an NFL player."

Sample Prompts that Relate to Personal Purposes for Reading

"Oh, yeah, I read this author's last novel. I bet this is good too because ___."

"I need something light and funny to read, and this title and cover look fun because ___."

"I'm just learning to cook, and I can tell by the ingredients and directions that this is too advanced for me right now because ___."

"This may connect to my interest in/study of ___."

"Reading this may help me to find out whether there are any rattlesnakes in this area of the country and other things like ___."

"Reading this may help me to understand what breaks up some relationships ___."

"Reading this may help me to understand what it was like to be a foot soldier in the Civil War ___."

2. Make Predictions

As you begin reading, begin predicting what will come next. Correct and revise predictions as you gain information from the text.

PROMPTS FOR LOCAL-LEVEL PREDICTIONS

"I'm guessing that ___ will happen next." "I bet that ___ ." "I wonder if ___ ."

Examples

"I'm guessing that he will be captured by the guards looking for deserters."

"I'll bet that there are no rattlesnakes in Maine because it is too cold there."

PROMPTS FOR GLOBAL PREDICTIONS

"I think this book will be about [the general topic of …] I wonder if ___. I imagine the
   author believes___. I think the tone of the book will be… [sad, happy in the end,
   pessimistic] about human beings___."

Examples

"I bet the author fought in the war and that he will be against wars because of his experiences."

"I'm guessing that this book will be about why the Vikings disappeared."

"*Pobby and Dingan* will be sad because it starts with her friends being maybe-dead."

3. Connect Personally

Show how you use your own experience to help make meaning, and the ways you bring
your experiences of other texts to help you understand this one. I call this "relating life
to literature" or "bringing life to text." Beth Davey calls this process the "like a ___"
step, when readers say to themselves, *This is like when Joey and I went fishing* or *This is
just like that movie I saw.*

   I also ask students to practice the reverse operation, considering how they might
apply what they are reading to their life. I call this "relating literature to life" or "text-to-
life connections."

PROMPTS

"This is like_____" "This reminds me of _____ ." "This could help me with ____ ."

   "This is helping me with/to think about/to make plans for _____."

Examples

"This story is like a software game I know called Diablo 2."

"This is like the time that we went on a ferry to Nova Scotia."

"This book is organized in the same way as that one I read about reptiles, so I can
expect that each picture will be followed by a description."

"This is helping me make plans for building a robot with Legos."

4. Visualize

Show how you take the sensory and physical details the author gives you and expand them
in your mind's eye to create an image or a scene. As I've said, this ability to "see" what one is
reading, to create accurate mental models and/or sensory-rich story worlds as one reads is
crucial to engaged reading. Demonstrate how you develop and adapt images as you read,
whether it's an expression on a character's face, the interaction of resistors and charges in an
electrical circuit, the workings of an engine, the room the characters are in, and so on.

PROMPTS

"In my mind's eye," "I imagine," "I see _____ ." or "I have a picture of _____ ."

Examples

"In my mind's eye I see a girl entering a dark room."

"I see a scientist working at his desk."

"I imagine a floor plan of the house, and I can see how it is organized with the kitchen
in the back with a bay window."

"In my head I can see an electrical circuit plan and I see where these lightbulbs would
go in that circuit and how the battery pushes the charges."

5. Monitor Comprehension

Demonstrate how expert readers constantly (though subconsciously) monitor comprehension by asking, "Does this make sense?" Show that you expect what you read to
make sense to you and that if it doesn't you will stop to identify this as a problem.

PROMPTS

"This is (not) making sense because _____." "This is (not) what I expected because _____."

"This connects (or doesn't) to what I already read/already know because _____."

Examples

"This doesn't make sense to me because before it said there were three soldiers and now there are only two."

"This isn't what I expected because it was about electrical circuitry and now it is about something called resistors."

"This isn't making sense because my mind was drifting for the last several paragraphs so I'll have to go back and reread _____."

"This doesn't make sense because I don't know what the word *conjoin* means, and it seems they're talking about that."

"This connects to what I read before about how the Vikings navigated because it shows how they kept exploring."

6. Use Fix-Up Strategies to Address Confusion and Repair Comprehension

Repairing one's confusion comes just a heartbeat after Step 5, of course. Demonstrate how you use various strategies when you can't grasp something or wish to check your understanding. Emphasize that even expert readers sometimes run into texts they have difficulty reading, or can't read. But when they do, they address these problems by:

* rereading
* reading ahead to see if that will clear things up
* reviewing and synthesizing previous ideas from the text and relating these "chunks" of concepts to the confusing ideas
* replacing a word or words they don't know with one(s) that they know and think would make sense in this context; looking up a word in the dictionary
* changing their ideas or visualization of the story to match new information, i.e. you may find that how you have visualized the story or what you think the text is really about is in error, and you need to make a self-correction, radically reconceiving your ideas
* asking someone for help

PROMPTS

"Maybe I'd better _____." "Something I could do is _____." "Since I don't understand this word, a good strategy would be to _____." "First I saw, but now I see _____." "What I thought this was about no longer makes sense because _____." "I need to revise my thinking by _____." "Maybe I need to consider _____."

Examples

"Maybe I'd better read on for a few paragraphs to see if I can make this clearer to myself."

"I don't understand how this fits with what came before, so something I could do is reread the previous passage to see if I can make the connection."

"Since I don't understand this word, a good strategy would be to use the context and make a guess and see if that works."

"I thought this was about paying taxes but the detail about using enough detergent doesn't make sense so maybe I need to consider that this is about doing the laundry."

THE MOVES MAKE THE READER

These general process reading moves are powerful, giving kids a way to use general processes that are basic to all reading tasks and applicable to all kinds of texts. They are particularly valuable, eye opening, and, dare I say, life changing, for our students who struggle most. One of my favorite stories is about Jon, who after hearing a classmate's think-aloud emoted, "I can't believe you do all that stuff when you read! Holy crap, I'm not doing… like nothing… compared to you." His classmate Ron, a teammate on the wrestling team, concluded a long commentary by saying, "If you don't do all that when you read, then you're not reading! It's like wrestling, man, you have to be there! You have to know the moves and make the moves! If you just sit there you'll get pinned to the mat!"

Jon decided to "borrow" Ron's strategies and reading moves, and by doing so he became a more competent reader.

After engaging in his first few think-alouds, another reluctant reader implored, "Why didn't someone tell me that this is what readers do?" his voice loud with anger. When I asked him why he was so upset, he said, "If I had known what to do, I would have done it!" Then he added, "Why didn't you tell us this before? Is it supposed to be a big secret or something?" "What bugs me," he continued, "is that it's really not so hard…. I guess I really didn't need to go through all that suffering and feeling stupid."

Think-alouds ensure that the hallmarks of engaged reading don't remain a big secret to a single child in our classrooms.

CHAPTER 3

AUTHOR'S CRAFT, READER'S ROLE:
Using Free-Response and Cued Think-Alouds to Show the Link Between These Processes

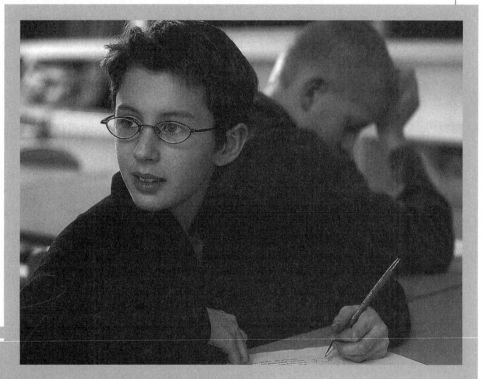

Fiona responds to cues that prompt her to ask different types of questions as she composes her think-aloud.

I n this chapter, I'll highlight ways to use think-alouds to help students understand
how they currently read and to take on specific new reading strategies. Then we'll
do a "free think-aloud" during which readers report out everything they are aware
of doing as they read. This method is great for giving students—and you—a kind of
panoramic view of their reading process. Students see how they read, share their characteristic ways of reading with classmates, recognize that others read differently from the
way they do, and realize that expert readers call upon a wide variety of strategies at the
same time—strategies that they may wish to appropriate and use for themselves. In
sum, it helps them appreciate how complex expert reading can be and to see where they
might proceed next as readers.

We'll then turn to "cued think-alouds." With these, you guide students to notice
certain things about a text and an author's craft. You'll use these think-alouds when you
want to develop students' ability to notice particular features of text and then apply
particular strategies to interpret them.

FREE RESPONSES: WHEN AND HOW TO USE THEM

A free-response think-aloud is indeed free—it's a freewheeling monologue wherein a reader
reports on everything she can about what she is thinking, doing, seeing, feeling, asking, and
noticing as she reads. Instead of focusing only on general-process strategies of reading (as we
did in Chapter 2), now we're interested in hearing every move a reader makes.

I often use this kind of think-aloud with students. It gives them a fast, big picture
of all the activities readers engage in, and it gives me information that helps me plan
my instruction. I learn what they do and don't do as readers.

BEGINNING-OF-YEAR BASELINE
I like to have each of my students do such a think-aloud early in the year so that I can
see how they read—their typical modes of response, what strategies they use and fail to
use, and so on. Many of my students can report very little awareness about their reading processes. This is important information for me as I plan instruction for self-monitoring (see Chapter 4) and it provides a baseline against which I can measure their subsequent growth as readers.

I often like to conclude a unit or a course with a free-response think-aloud because it brings together all the processes we have studied, and demonstrates how expert readers integrate their use of multiple strategies into a rich reading of text. Having students do such a think-aloud can also serve as an excellent evaluation tool (see Chapter 7).

END-OF-YEAR MEASURE OF GROWTH

It's also great to use a free response think-aloud near the end of the year to show students how they have added to their cache of reading strategies throughout the year. Comparisons with earlier think-alouds can be especially illuminating!

Chloe: Learning to Deepen the Questions

Ninth-grader Chloe's first free think-aloud of *The Incredible Journey* consisted solely of questions; she had interrogated the text, ripping into it like a homicide detective with literal questions like: Where is the story taking place? What kind of industry is there? What is John Longridge doing? Why does he have the animals with him?

When we reviewed her think-aloud, which I'd had her write in her notebook, I asked her to characterize how she had read this passage. "It's all questions," she replied.

"Where did you learn to ask these kinds of questions?" I asked her.

"In school," she succinctly replied. I agreed with her assessment, and it unfortunately demonstrates how school often works to impoverish students' views of reading and their use of reading strategies. Chloe was using the simplest and least useful kinds of questions, and not accidentally, those most often used at the end of chapters in a textbook.

I explained to Chloe that all her questions were literal questions, the answers to which could be found directly stated "right there" in the book. I told her these were necessary, but that authors expect their readers to go well beyond literal comprehension by asking and answering many other kinds of questions too.

I then introduced Chloe to Taffy Raphael's (1982) four kinds of QAR (question-answer relationship) questions, which include the literal "right-there" questions, but also include "think-and-search" inferring questions, "author-and-me" questions that connect personal experience to the text, and "on-your-own" questions about life and the world in general, which are stimulated by the book but which aren't necessarily answered in the book. I told Chloe that to appreciate a book to its fullest, readers have to use information from their personal lives, from the world, from other texts they've read, and from the current text as they read, and that asking these different kinds of QAR questions helps readers to use these various information sources. Expert readers use self-to-text, world-to-text, and text-to-text connections constantly as they read.

I prompted Chloe to use the models I'd provided to ask a think-and-search question of *The Incredible Journey* and she did so: "Why is the dog so miserable?"

"You've got it!" I cheered. "Now remember, that kind of question implies a certain

QARs

Taffy Raphael teases apart the myriad questions good readers pose as they read into four basic categories. The goal for us as teachers is to guide students to internalize posing these questions automatically as they read, as they reflect on their reading, and as they discuss books with others.

"IN THE TEXT" QUESTIONS

"Right-There" Questions: These are factual questions for which the answer is immediately available (directly stated) in the text. e.g., [In Katherine Paterson's *The Great Gilly Hopkins*] Where does Gilly Hopkins put the bubble gum that she takes out of her mouth?
How does Mrs. Ellis describe Gilly's new foster mother, Maime Trotter?
Think-and-Search Questions: These questions prompt readers to infer. A good reader poses the question to herself

(thinks), and then pieces together details from several places in the text (searches) to arrive at an answer (an inference). A reader often "searches" by reviewing in her mind what she's read, but at times will literally search, rereading pages or flipping ahead to find evidence for her hunch. Sometimes readers must fill in important gaps in the text by connecting information that occurs both before and after the gap.
e.g., Why does Gilly behave the way that she does?
Why does Mr. Randolph think the house will now be more lively?
Why does Gilly believe that her mother will come to get her?

"IN YOUR HEAD" QUESTIONS

Author-and-Me Questions: These questions require readers to connect their own life experiences and beliefs with details from the text. To answer such questions the reader must have read the text, but must also go action you have to take to find the answer. How do you know this is a think-and-search question?"

Chloe took a deep breath. "Because I have to make an educated guess, and because the clues to why he's sad are scattered around the chapter. I have to search, think, and put things together."

"Brava!" I clapped. "You asked an inference question! Authors want you to literally comprehend what they write, but they also want you to do some work, like putting details from throughout the chapter

beyond the text and bring her personal lived experiences to bear. A reader must make a personal connection between textual details and events and her own personal knowledge. e.g., How would I react to Gilly if I were Trotter, or William Ernest, or if I were living in the house with her? What does the author want me to think about Gilly's reactions to Trotter's house and to Mr. Randolph? How are my own prejudices similar or different from those of Gilly? What experiences of acceptance, rejection, or rebellion have I had that are similar or that contrast to Gilly's experiences?

On Your Own Questions: These questions are usually stirred by the events, topics, or theme of the text. However, the answer to this kind of question does not reside in the text. Rather, it comes from the reader thinking about the book's issues in a much wider context—not the world of the text, but the world. e.g., What are the causes of and solutions

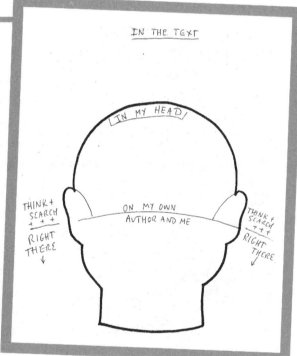

Students can use this graphic to fill in different kinds of questions about a passage as they read it.

to prejudice? For what reasons do children go into foster care? How would it feel to be in foster care? How would it feel to move around all the time? How might foster care programs be improved?

together to build a sense of character, or to figure out a pattern or answer a question, like why the dog is miserable!"

I then prompted her to ask an "author-and-me" question, and Chloe asked, "Why does the author want me to know that the dog is miserable?"

This one-on-one work helped Chloe to build on her strength and predisposition to question as she read. I also gave her some prompts to help her visualize as she read, and had her do a visual think-aloud (see Chapter 5) so that she would develop other visualizing skills she didn't currently use.

Branwin: Learning to Read Like a Writer

Like Chloe, seventh-grader Branwin's free response was overly dependent on one reading strategy. Branwin leaned heavily on making personal associations, such as "our house is painted white too." Or "I just learned the word for 'white' in German class." She ignored key story details, including the title, if she could not find a personal association for it. I praised her for bringing her personal background to a text as all expert readers do, and then nudged her to go beyond personal associations, to attend to story clues with a wider array of tools, in ways that an author might expect of her instead of solely in her personal, idiosyncratic way.

In our conference, we talked about features of a text that authors might expect us to notice. I knew she liked to write, so I used a piece she had written as an entry point. We looked at her latest story about her cat, and I asked what she had written there that she wanted her readers to pay attention to. "The title," she said, biting her lip.

"Yes!" I responded. "Authors always expect us to notice their titles— that's even called a 'rule of notice'!"

"And . . . I wanted them to notice how I didn't like my cat in the beginning."

"But you never said that! So how would they know? What clues would they have to notice?"

"How I played with my dog when my dad brought the cat home," she responded.

In this way, I guided Branwin to see that in addition to noticing details that she could relate to personally, she had to be on the lookout for other details the author had selected, and she had to try to figure out what the author intended. Just as she "coded" her own writing in certain ways, so do all authors.

Free-Response Think-aloud: An Example

To give you a look at a teacher-modeled free-response think-aloud in action, here is the opening of the short story "The Chaser" by John Collier, along with my report out as I read it aloud. My students and I discussed this story as part of a unit about love and relationships that explores the question, "What makes a good relationship?"

TEXT	THINK-ALOUD
The Chaser	**The title could refer to the drink you use to chase your first drink. Maybe it has a double meaning?**
Alan Austen, as nervous as a kitten, went up certain dark and creaky stairs	**Oh, very gothic. Everything dark and creaky. This is supposed to be scary. When you get dark and creaky you know you are in for some scares. This reminds me of those old Frankenstein movies.**
in the neighborhood of Pell Street,	**Am I supposed to know where Pell Street is? Is that important? Sounds like Pell Mell, like somebody is in a hurry, or like Pill, maybe this place is drug infested,**
and peered about for a long time at the dim landing before he found the name he wanted written obscurely on one of the doors.	**So he's never been here before and has come for a specific purpose. Why is the name so obscure? Has the person been here a long time, or maybe he does not want to be found unless someone is really looking for him and knows he's there.**
He pushed open this door, as he had been told to do,	**Without knocking? That's weird. So he's expected.**
and found himself in a tiny room, which contained no furniture but a plain kitchen table, a rocking chair, and an ordinary chair.	**Pretty empty and dumpy. I can really see this in my mind. The empty room, the table and two chairs.**

TEXT	THINK-ALOUD
On one of the dirty, buff-colored walls were a couple of shelves, containing in all perhaps a dozen bottles and jars.	**I can see the room even better know. Dirty brown walls and shelves. I'll bet these bottles and jars are important. It looks grimy though. I wonder if what is in those bottles is safe, approved by the FDA and all that. I think NOT!**
An old man sat in the rocking chair, reading a newspaper. Alan, without a word, handed him the card he had been given.	**Who gave it to him? Alan's obviously been sent here by someone.**
"Sit down, Mr. Austen," said the old man very politely. "I am glad to make your acquaintance."	**Very polite old geezer. He's formal. Educated. That doesn't match the crummy surroundings. I wonder if he really lives here. Or this is just where he does business?**
"Is it true," asked Alan, "that you have a certain mixture that has—er—quite extraordinary effects?"	**Oh, we get right to the point. This is what Alan has come for. I wonder what exactly he wants and why it is so important to him. I wonder if he is an addict or something.**
"My dear sir," replied the old man, "my stock in trade is not very large—I don't deal in laxatives and teething mixtures—	**Yeah, you wouldn't come to some run down scary place to buy laxatives. Alan wants something you can't buy elsewhere, something sneaky and illegal.**
but such as it is, it is varied. I think nothing I sell has effects which could be precisely described as "ordinary."	**So he sells things that are "extraordinary." I wonder what that could be? I'll have to read on to find out!**

After I "think-aloud" the story, students can identify the various cues I attended to, such as the title, the setting, the characters; and what I tried to figure out, e.g. what is the story really about, why is Alan here and what does he want; and the various strategies I used, such as predicting, asking questions, visualizing, and bringing meaning forward with me as I read.

In this way, we can identify the variety of things expert readers do as they read, and can identify what students are doing or might do as they read. We could also compare think-alouds of the same story and see what they might have noticed and done that I did not. This could lead to discussing what was lost and gained by making particular moves.

Free-response think-alouds can be used in a variety of ways, but the general point is to highlight and consider the meaning-making activity of the reader in ways that will inform future reading.

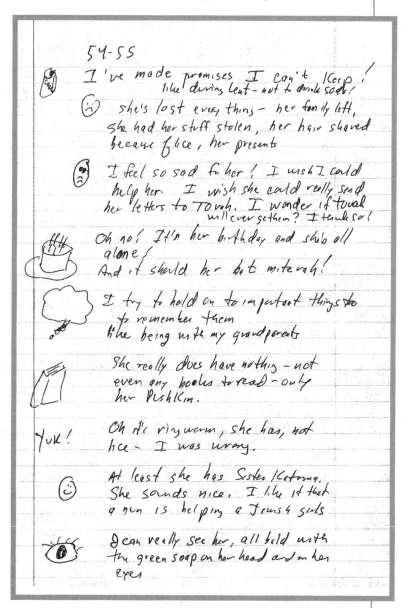

This is Katrina's free response to pages 54 and 55 of *Letters from Rifka* by Karen Hesse. She coded her responses with illustrations.

Prompts That Guide Students' Reflection on Free Response

You can use questions like these to stimulate discussion during reporting out, or give them to students when you want them to reflect on their think-aloud by writing.

- Characterize your reading of this passage. How did you personally read this; was it visual, like watching a movie? Did you ask a lot of questions, was your think-aloud transcript like an interview of the text? Did you make a lot of predictions? Did you make a lot of personal connections? Was it emotional?

- Why do you think you read the passage in this particular way? What did you learn about yourself from the think aloud? What kinds of things grabbed your attention or interested you and what does that tell about you?

- What did you learn about others in your group? How did they respond and what did you learn about them from their responses?

- What did you learn about how you read? What did you notice about how you read? About what you do and don't do? About how you compared to the other readers in your group?

- What did you learn from your group members about other ways of reading? What other strategies or ways of responding did group members use that you might want to try out?

- What did you learn about the text, how it works and what it means? What new insights or ideas about the story came up that you didn't notice when you read on your own?

- What did you learn about the text topic/unit topic/inquiry question? How might we use this text to think about this topic?

CUED THINK-ALOUDS: WHEN AND HOW TO USE THEM

During this same inquiry unit about relationships, I decided that I now wanted to zero in on a particular strategy that I think is central to the unit: inferring character. In fact, it's not merely a reading strategy that will help my students pursue the goals of our unit; it's a life strategy that is important to their future success and happiness as individuals. Knowing how to infer character helps us decide whom to trust, whom to hire, whom to vote for in an election, and assists us in myriad other real-life situations.

Let's also say that I know my students find inferring character somewhat challenging. (It's in their zone of proximal development.) Knowing this, I don't want to overwhelm them with all the things readers do; I want to focus my instruction solely on inferring character. As I do this, I will cue text features that I believe the author coded into the text so that readers can infer character. The literary theorist Peter Rabinowitz calls these codings "rules of notice" (see box, page 80). There are general rules of notice, and then there are rules of notice for particular tasks (like reading symbolism) or texts (like reading fables). Here we'll concentrate on general rules of notice and on special ones for reading and understanding character.

To help students notice these codes, I initially provide assistance by underlining such features and asking students to be sure to respond to all or some of these as they read. As we move along the instructional continuum, I'll ask groups of students to underline the codes during group work, and later I will have them work alone to do so.

To highlight rules of notice and how a reader is expected to interpret them, I may think-aloud in front of students in the following way. Notice the underlining of significant coded text features:

TEXT	THINK-ALOUD
The Chaser	**I know that titles are something we are supposed to notice. (Rule of notice—titles are very important to story meaning. If they refer to a character, the title is important to understanding the character or tells us to pay attention to the character.) I wonder if the Chaser is a person, like someone chasing somebody or something, or whether it refers to the drink you use to chase down another drink. If it's a character then it will be important that he is chasing something, probably something he really wants.**

TEXT	THINK-ALOUD
Alan Austen,	**(Rule of Notice—names are important, nicknames even more so.) This guy's initials are AA, like in Alcoholics Anonymous. Maybe he's a drinker and the title is about drinking. Or maybe this is just a common name for a common guy. I'll have to read more.**
as nervous as a kitten,	**(Rule of notice—when a character is introduced, this is important. First impressions are the most lasting.) So I am supposed to know this guy is a "scaredy cat," ha-ha-ha. I see him as kind of wimpy.**
went up certain dark and creaky stairs in the neighborhood of Pell Street, and peered about for a long time at the dim landing before he found the name he wanted written obscurely on one of the doors.	**(Rule of notice—the most important and privileged parts of a text are the beginning and the end. So I need to pay attention to what is being suggested here about this guy.) Yes, I think I am right about this being a regular guy who is kind of a wimp. I see him slowly and carefully going up the stairs, wishing he wasn't there because it is dark and creaky. I wonder why he is there anyway?**
He pushed open this door, as he had been told to do,	**Ah, so this is the kind of guy who does what other people tell him. He doesn't really take control of his life.**
and found himself in a tiny room, which contained no furniture but a plain kitchen table, a rocking chair, and an ordinary chair. On one of the dirty, buff-colored walls were a couple of shelves, containing in all perhaps a dozen bottles and jars.	**(Rule of notice—a character's surroundings reveal character.) This place is a dive. There's hardly anything in it. I wonder if this guy lives here or uses it as an office. The rocking chair is for him because he waits around for people. The other chair is for people like Alan who visit him. This guy must be a slum landlord or something.**

An old man sat in the rocking chair, reading a newspaper. Alan, without a word, handed him the card he had been given. "Sit down, Mr. Austen," said the old man very politely. "I am glad to make your acquaintance."	(Rule of Notice: Any time something is surprising, or there is a sudden change, pay attention.) I am surprised at this guy's politeness. It doesn't seem to fit the crummy surroundings at all. Makes me wonder why he is here in a place where someone refined seems so out of place.
"Is it true," asked Alan, "that you have a certain mixture that has—er—quite extraordinary effects?"	(Rule of notice—When a character speaks for the first time, pay attention. The way a character talks, what they talk about, the words they use, etc. all help reveal character.) Alan is beside himself with urgency. He can't wait to get to the point. But he can't spit out what the mixture is for… Is it poison? Is it magical? What does he want with it?
"My dear sir," replied the old man, "my stock in trade is not very large—I don't deal in laxatives and teething mixtures—but such as it is, it is varied. I think nothing I sell has effects which could be precisely described as 'ordinary'."	(Rule of notice—when something surprising or out of the ordinary or unexpected happens, pay attention! Anytime expectations are ruptured, look for an explanation. If it happens to a character, we are getting to see something special and important about them.) The old coot is playing coy. I bet he knows what Alan is talking about; after all, someone referred Alan to him. But he's not telling Alan what he wants to know, except that everything he sells is extraordinary. It's kind of surprising to me that this guy sells extraordinary stuff in such shabby surroundings. I wonder what's up. Something shady is going on. This Alan has passed into the criminal underworld because he wants something so bad, I'll bet.

After such an activity, we would reflect on and name the kinds of things we need to notice when we infer character. We could come up with a list like this:

RULES OF NOTICE

(based on the work of Peter Rabinowitz in *Before Reading*)

GENERAL RULES OF NOTICE

Remember to notice and interpret the meaning of the following:

Titles

Beginnings

Climaxes/Key Details

Extended Descriptions

Changes, e.g., in Direction, Setting, Point of View

Repetition

Surprises and Ruptures

Endings

RULES OF NOTICE FOR CHARACTER

Titles: Pay attention to titles! Does this title tell us who to pay attention to or something we should know about a character or what will happen to her?

Names and Nicknames: The names and particularly the nicknames of characters are almost always important and reveal something about the characters.

Introductions: Pay attention when characters are introduced!

Problems: Pay attention to any problem the character might have or a challenge they are facing.

Actions: Typical activities as well as actions they take and decisions they make reveal character.

Physical Description: Physical features and how they are described.

Clothing: What they wear, styles.

Way they talk/language they use: Dialects, tone, correctness, language used.

Typical setting or surroundings: Where do they hang out, how do they decorate their room, where do they feel comfortable or uncomfortable?

Friends or people they hang with: What company do they choose to keep?

What others say about them: What do people who know the character say about him?

Tastes/likes/dislikes: What particular tastes, attitudes, feelings, beliefs, soapbox opinions or antipathies does the character express?

Character thoughts: What do we learn about the character from her private thoughts, fears, desires?

Character changes: Changes in a character are always important! If a character changes it is for a reason and the author wants us to figure out what the reason is. This will probably have something to do with the author's generalization or theme of the story.

CUED THINK-ALOUD: AN EXAMPLE

After modeling and asking students to help identify and use cues (in this case, for infer-ring character), it's time for them to start using and interpreting the cues in small groups if they need the support, or on their own if they are ready. When some fifth graders I was working with had reached this point, I conducted the following class.

"All right!" I announced to my students. "All you blue-collar scholars have just finished reading Avi's *The Fighting Ground*. Since it was only a week ago, you'll definitely remember doing a cued think-aloud of the first chapter. I cued you to pay attention to what? Robby?"

Superstudent Robby crisply replied, "To Jonathan's character—what he was like and what we thought about him." Robby's answer was so efficient that I thought he might even add a military *"Sir!"* to his answer and give me a salute. I've always been a dreamer because in Maine no one gets called "Sir," just "Bub" or "Hey, you!" if you're lucky.

"Excellent, Robby!" I said. "Now we are going to do a cued think-aloud of the last chapter. But as you do it, I want *you* to underline the character cues and respond to them. And when you are done, we are going to compare Jonathan at the beginning and the end of the book, see if he's changed, explain why or why not, and try to figure out what Avi is trying to tell us about the kind of experience Jonathan just went through and how it might affect people."

The kids all yelled "Yeah!" gave each other high-fives and got immediately to work. Oh, no, I'm dreaming again. At any rate, I passed out photocopies of the last chapter, arranged on the left-hand side of the page so they could write their think-aloud on the right side. They did get quietly to work, but without the pregame hoopla. Oh, well. Some students who were still struggling a bit worked together under my supervision, but most of the class worked independently.

Here's the very end of Robby's think-aloud effort:

TEXT	THINK-ALOUD
…Jonathan understood that his father's fear had not been for himself.	**In the beginning J. thought his dad was a wimp, that everyone was a wimp. Now he understands his dad was afraid for him, not for himself. This is a definite change because now he understands something he didn't before, and he understands why his father was afraid, because of the boy he found whose parents were dead.**

TEXT	THINK-ALOUD
And suddenly, Jonathan <u>understood more.</u>	**See, he keeps seeing and understanding things he didn't because now he's actually seen the war and how bad it is. He's really changed. Well , his attitude has changed and maybe that's the most important thing.**
Understood the most important thing— that <u>he had indeed been spared.</u>	**See, he's thinking all this. Before, he thought people died because they weren't smart enough or couldn't shoot well enough. Now he knows he's wrong and he knows he should have died. He would have never thought all this before. He sees he's not unbeatable and that bad things can happen even if you don't deserve it.**
Oh, how <u>glad he was to be there.</u>	**Ha, this is a change. A day ago he was totally bored to be here. All he wanted was to go fight. He thought home was the pits!**
And <u>Alive.</u>	**Yeah, now he sees war is about death, not all the glory he kept talking about in Chapter One. I just noticed that everything on this last page is about Jonathan and how he changed. I guess Mr. Avi is trying to drive a point home to us about how much you can change in one day.**
<u>Oh, Alive.</u>	**Yeah, yeah, yeah, Mr. Avi. I get it. The kid is really glad to be alive and he never thought about being alive or dead before.**

A cued think-aloud draws the students' attention to the author's important codings, to all the inner thoughts, details, and seemingly unimportant asides that, if missed, can thwart comprehension and dampen one's engagement with a book. Through the think-aloud, the student is required to "slow his speed" and respond to all these textual cues.

In this case, my students were experienced in identifying and responding to character cues, so I asked them to identify these cues on their own and then respond. It's interesting that Robby recognizes that the whole last page is a series of cues about Jonathan's changed character. He even directly addresses "Mr. Avi" and how he as the author is making his point! (An author-and-me kind of response.)

This activity was a great lead-in to a whole-class discussion about how and why Jonathan had changed and how this helped express the point or theme of the book. Doing the think-aloud, sharing them with each other, the class discussion, and a final writing activity about Jonathan's character change were all completed during one forty-minute period.

Since the class was working on argumentation (see Chapter 6), I used the text-specific processes of argument to frame their response and then had them code their claim, evidence and explanations after they had written their piece.

A Student's Think-Aloud–Based Written Response

At the beginning of the book Jonathan's highest value was feeling alive and at the end this value had not changed, it was still feeling alive. What had changed was what made him feel alive. This was totally different, as will be revealed! (Claim) The great Robby-ini will reveal all to those with the intelligence to understand!

In the beginning, Jonathan needed adventure to feel alive. He was tired of the same old things, of working on the farm. He wanted adventure. He wanted to fight in the war. He wanted something bigger and more important than just farming. All this evidence is in the first few chapters. (Evidence) This shows he felt he wasn't as alive as he could be and he wanted to be more alive, more on the edge, taking more risks, getting more from life. (Explanation)

At the end of the book he has totally had it with the war, people being killed, people being stupid, being hungry and cold. When he finally gets home it says "How glad he was to be there" so his attitude has totally changed about the farm and his family. Then it says, "And alive. Oh, Alive." (Evidence) You see he's glad to be home because it is safe. And he can live there without being killed or afraid of being killed. He realizes that this is what life is all about, not about extreme sports and all that and risking your life all the time. (Explanation) So his highest value is the same, but what makes him feel alive is different. In the beginning he wants action; at the end he wants to be the same and be with his family who loves him. (More explanation) So what makes him feel alive is different from being in the battle.

MORE THINK-ALOUD SCAFFOLDING FOR PARTICULAR STRATEGY USE

 STUDENTS DO/TEACHER HELPS

Say Something Game for Pairs and Small Groups

If, after modeling and discussion, my students still have difficulty interpreting the underlined features of a cued think-aloud, I might ask them to play a version of Say Something (a game I learned from my friend Kylene Beers) that gives them practice summarizing. To compose a summary, readers must notice key details (codes the author wants them to notice), interpret their meaning, and string these details together into a coherent whole. The game itself is a teacher-sponsored kind of scaffolding, and as the students' work is articulated I have the chance to intervene and assist them.

To begin, I have students work in pairs or small groups. I give them all the same passage of text from a book or novel we are reading, and one student reads the passage aloud. Then another student in that group has to "say something" that comes to mind, and then the first student or another student chimes in. At first, students tend to make statements about anything at all. But as they become proficient, I ask them to say something that cites a key detail and how they interpret that detail.

Group members can record these statements and then link them together to compose a summary of the

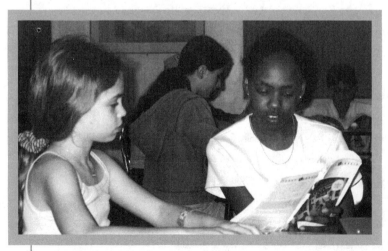
Two students work together as they read and play "Say Something."

complete passage. Ultimately, all the key details should have been articulated so that the summary is complete. It's important that everyone in the group collaborate to decide what all the key details mean in terms of a main idea or author's generalization.

It's important to note that students may need help identifying topics and key details and how these contribute to story meaning and an author's generalization. (See Chapter 6 for more on this task-specific process.)

Say Something Specific: Underline Text for Greater Scaffolding

For students who still need to be prompted to notice the appropriate cues for the strategy and interpretive operations being studied, I've developed another version of the game in which students say something in response to cues I've underlined in the text. Working in groups, students say aloud what they were doing and thinking when they read the underlined textual cues. Each group member says something for each cue, and the order in which they do so can revolve with each cue. Everyone has to "say something" when it is their turn. Even if they weren't doing or thinking anything, they are cued to try to come up with something. Anything will do, even "I wasn't doing anything." As group members share responses, they are teaching each other how to deal with the cues authors leave them as they use particular meaning-making strategies. This version of the game can also involve summarizing and then basing an authorial generalization on the summary, as shown below. In this transcript, students are playing Say Something with underlined codes for inferring character from the end of "The Chaser." Using underlined codes keeps students focused on the task or text-specific process being studied, and insures that they are directed to report out about these particular processes. In this case, Joe is playing the role of secretary who records and will report on his group's think-aloud.

TEXT	THINK-ALOUD
"She will care intensely. <u>You'll be her sole interest in life."</u>	**Anna:** YUK. It's not her who will care about him, it's some drugged-up dope. It's just the love potion that will make her love him. She won't be herself. This is what kills me. He wants to drug her up so he can be loved, not so she can love him or he can love her. What a jerk!!! **Joe:** Yeah, right. What she said.

> Tish: Say something of your own, Joe! It's the rule!
>
> Joe: Uh, I don't think it's so bad for him [Alan] to be her sole interest. The old guy doesn't think so either... he's using that to sell the stuff.
>
> Anna: You are so screwed up!
>
> Joe: If girls paid a little more attention to guys then we... I mean he... wouldn't be in this position. We're nice to you ladies and what do we get in return??
>
> Tish: You are so yuk-luk!
>
> Joe: Okay, you say something:
>
> Tish: Anna's right. This Alan schmo is only looking out for himself. That's why he listens to a sexist pig like the Old Man. They see women as things to own.... No, they see them as pets and you have to train your pets to behave like you want. That's why he says this and that's what the author wants us to see—they are both sexist pigs.
>
> Joe: Enough already!
>
> Tish: What are the key details to remember from this section?
>
> Anna: The potion will make her completely change and think only about Alan.
>
> Joe: I think we ought to include that she'll be jealous.
>
> Anna: When I said she completely changes, that covers that.
>
> Joe: (mumbles)
>
> Tish: Write it down, Joe, you are the secretary!

[Story reading and Say Something continues to the story's conclusion.]

Bringing It All Together: Whole-Class Reporting Out

When students have finished small group spoken think-alouds, such as the ones students did for "The Chaser," I often ask them to report out to the larger group what they have learned. This can be done quite quickly, and it often leads to rich discussion of strategy use, the text, or the topic of study.

For example, after we did a "Say Something" for "The Chaser," students wrote what they learned about inferring character and about the story through their think-aloud discussions. The next day we reported out, recorded insights on the overhead, and still had time to do some drama activities inspired by the story. When reporting out, questions and concerns are often voiced; new insights and developing strategies are often shared. I might use prompts (see box below) to guide the reporting out.

Again, structuring this kind of reflection into collaborative lessons helps students consolidate their learning and move ever closer to applying it to new situations. Our ultimate goal, of course, is for students to independently evaluate and adapt their own reading procedures. The reading process must be adapted in specific ways when engaged in task- or text-specific processes. I'll explore how to direct students to use and report out on several of these kinds of specific processes in much greater detail in Chapter 6. And of course, being able to self-report their strategy use enables students to self-assess and self-correct their reading in ways which are central to any reading process. Reporting out in this way gives students guided practice in this kind of self-assessment (for more on Self-Assessment, see Chapter 7).

SUPPORTING STUDENTS BEFORE, DURING, AND AFTER READING

It's vital to embed your think-alouds within an instructional framework designed to assist readers before, during, and after reading a text. Think-alouds are one tool of many you will use; others include drama scenarios, written reflections, key questions, and so on. Think-alouds can be combined nicely with these other kinds of activities. Taken together, these practices can be integrated into what is called a directed reading and thinking activity (Stauffer, 1969). Following is a blueprint to help you build your own DRTAs, then an example of a DRTA I created for "The Chaser."

GUIDELINES FOR CREATING A DIRECTED READING AND THINKING ACTIVITY (DRTA)

(adapted from Wilhelm, Baker and Dube, 2001)

Before Teaching: Set your teaching purposes

1. Set goals for your unit (or for a text you have chosen).

- Affective/attitudinal goal: What emotions and attitudes do I want to cultivate in my students?
- Conceptual goal: What content or substance do I want my students to attend to and remember?
- Procedural goal: How am I helping students to know *how* to do something new as readers? What textual codes am I helping them to notice, and what interpretive strategies am I helping them to use?

Effective Practices: Choose an appropriate text that is short and serves your teaching purposes. Focus on transferable goals that students can put to use immediately in new situations.

Before Reading: Motivate your students

2. Front-load to activate students' background knowledge and awaken personal connections.

- Purpose: What purpose might reading this text serve? How can I help students to adopt a personally relevant purpose?
- Personal connection: How can I connect students' interests, experiences, and needs to the text?
- Activate background knowledge: How can I activate personal background information and experiences that will be useful during reading?
- Build background knowledge: How can I build knowledge for students of important contexts, concepts, procedures, and vocabulary necessary to successfully comprehend this text?

Effective practices: Identifying topic of selection, brainstorming background knowledge, opinionairres, K-W-L, scenario rankings, drama, background research, etc. (for a full discussion of various motivational and frontloading techniques, please see *Strategic Reading*, 2001, Wilhelm, et. al.)

Beginning to Read: Preview, set purposes, enter the text

3. Support student entry into the text and the reading process.

- Preview entire text: How can I help students get a sense of the text's overall structure and/or genre?
- Read first section: How can I assist students to get into the text by reading together or in small groups?
- Making meaning: How can I help students to summarize important information and text cues and carry these forward as they read?
- Predicting: How can I help students make predictions about future action that will help motivate and drive their reading?
- Knowing purposes: How can I encourage students to reflect on their personal (and academic/theme) purposes for this reading?
- Making personal connections: How can I help students to associate the text with their own lives and experiences throughout their reading of the text?

Effective practices: Brainstorming/Round table discussion to identify class inquiry purpose, and individual reading purposes; look ahead to how text will be used after reading; teacher-modeled think-aloud, proceeding to whole-class, or small-group think-alouds; Say Something, drama strategies such as role-play, journal writing.

During Reading: Encourage a deeper and fuller experience of the text

4. Guide the reading.

- Navigating students' journey through the text: How can I cue, guide, and support students to notice key details, stated and implied relationships, structural demands, and textual conventions that are important to the strategies I am teaching them?
- Sustaining personal connections: How can I help them continue to make and reflect on their personal associations?
- Making text-to-world connections: How can I help them to engage with and learn content from the text that is important to our purposes?

Effective practices: Cued think-alouds, (sometimes cue text differently for different groups of students at different levels of ability); structured questions; drama strategies.

After Reading: Reflect on the textual experience

5. Take students back into the text.

• How can I help students reenter the text and reflect upon it alone and together?

• How can I help students to reflect on the constructedness and meaning of the text and reading experience?

Effective practices: Group think-alouds and reporting out; written reflections on their think-aloud and/or the content of the book; debates, discussions of themes, drama activities, reflective or analytical journal writing.

Follow-up: Extend understanding

6. Give a final assignment to synthesize a coherent view of the text as a whole and consider thematic generalizations that go beyond the text.

• Student inquiry projects or writing to encourage further connections, motivate further inquiry, go beyond the known to what may be unknown.

• Explore textual implications of "So What?" How can we use what we have learned or decided in our own life? How might what we have learned come into play in the future?

Effective practices: Design projects such as hypermedia or video documentaries, museum exhibits, drama activities like trial of character or conversation with author, explore "What If?" situations, elaborate on text, sequel writing, set goals for further inquiry.

DRTA FOR "THE CHASER"

1. Set Teaching Goals

a. To help students personally connect to the text, bringing their life experiences to the reading and taking the reading back to their life.

b. To explore our unit theme of "What makes a good relationship?"

c. To use character clues to understand characters and their contribution to story meaning.

2. Front-loading: Activating background; building personal connections

a. Drama scenario*: You've heard that there is a new pheromone-based perfume available on the black market. If you wear it around someone for an extended period and you are alone with them, they will begin to become delirious and think they are in love with you. You know you can get some of this stuff. What would you do? Role-play a discussion you are having with your best friend about the costs and benefits of buying and using such a perfume for your upcoming date with someone you really like but who isn't really returning your affection. (To rehearse students for the story and help them to achieve story entry.)

*My thanks to Michael Smith for the drama ideas.

b. How does someone act who is like a "kitten," who is "indifferent," who says "dear sir"? (Rule of notice: Pay attention to how people are introduced, how they act and speak.)

c. What adjective best describes the person you would want to spend your life with? Do they have to be this way naturally, or would it be okay if you helped to make them be this way? (Rehearse students to consider the purpose of reading the story. Is having freedom to choose part of a good relationship?)

d. For writing in your journal: Think of a time you really wanted something badly. What would you have done to get this valued thing? What would you not have done? Why did you draw the line where you did? Or do you wish you had drawn the line at a different place? Why? (Prepare students to converse about the story and whether what Alan is doing is okay—according to author, to themselves.)

3. Previewing and Purpose Setting: Helping kids achieve story entry, appropriate stance, begin meaning construction, and start predicting and hypothesizing

a. Why do you think the story is called "The Chaser"? (Rule of notice: Titles are always important to story meaning.)

b. Read the first five paragraphs of the story. What is your initial impression of Alan? Why do you think he is here in this apartment on Pell Street?

c. Why is the old man unnamed? What do you think it is that he does?

4. Guided Reading

a. Think-aloud—as you read, write down in the margins things you are thinking, feeling, seeing, doing, connecting to.

b. Respond to the underlined phrases. How do these phrases help us to understand the characters and illuminate story meaning? What kinds of things are underlined?

c. As you read, try to build meaning about the following:
   - How is this story about relationships?
   - What would be effective and ineffective about using the "love potion"?
   - Why do you think the old man keeps talking about the "cleaning fluid" and why is this so much more expensive? How does this demonstrate new information about the old man and his potions?
   - What points are being made about the theme of relationships?
   - How do the characters and their relationships, and the way the potion will change these, help to make these points?

5. Discussion and Rereading

a. Go through your think-aloud comments with some partners and search for repeated ideas and themes.

b. Revisit guided reading questions.

6. Following Up

a. Compose a personality profile of the old man for *People* magazine. State your opinion of this character and follow it with evidence from the story and what you infer from the story. What do you think about the "services" he provides?

b. Drama scenario: Put Alan and Diana on the "hot seat" and interview them about their relationship before the story starts, then right after the love potion is administered, then a year later. How have things changed? Prepare your answers first in small groups, then one of you will take the hot seat to answer questions from the rest of the class.

c. What will happen between Alan and Diana after the story ends? What does this show about the nature of good relationships? Is this what the author wants us to think? Do we agree with him?

CHAPTER 4

NAVIGATING MEANING:
Using Think-Alouds to Help Readers Monitor Comprehension

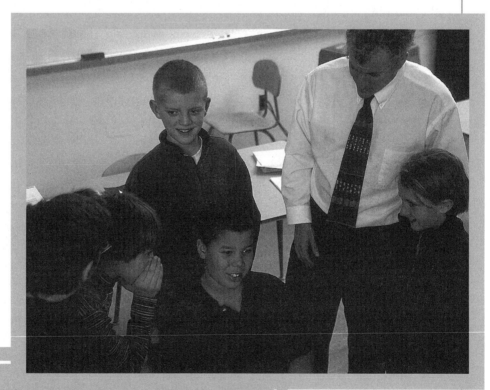

Students and teacher use a "forum" or "fishbowl" to help Douglass monitor his comprehension and use fix-up strategies.

The hallmark of an expert reader is that she actively and continually makes meaning as she reads. Whether reading a thirty-two page picture book or a seven hundred page Russian novel, an expert reader brings meanings forward as she reads each page and uses these meanings to inform her understanding of the unfolding text. She is eminently aware when her meaning-making begins to break down and has strategies to repair faltering comprehension.

Many research studies show that facility in monitoring comprehension distinguishes good readers from poor ones. Expert readers read on a global level, using individual words and local-level phrase- and sentence-meaning to construct a coherent picture of what a text is trying to express. Proficient readers are able to self-correct and fix comprehension problems as they read and have a goal in mind: understanding the larger meaning of a text.

Poorer readers, on the other hand, are often mired at the local level of comprehension as they concentrate on decoding words and sentences. They don't see how various parts of a whole text relate to each other and work together to create a larger meaning. They often have difficulty bringing the meaning of a word or sentence forward to the next sentence. Sometimes such students don't even seem to understand that reading goes beyond decoding words to making meanings with those words. And they don't see texts as parts of larger conversations—called grand conversations by many literacy educators—that are about important debates, issues, and intensely important human choices. They don't understand that by reading and then accepting, adapting, or rejecting what they have learned, they have entered into the grand social conversation that is reading, not only the reading of texts, but of using texts to "read" the world.

DECODING: WORDS, NOTHING BUT WORDS!

One of my favorite stories about this impoverished view of reading involves my seventh-grade student Marvin, a poor reader who could decode words. He'd spent lots of years in pull-out situations involving phonics and word-identification programs like DISTAR and the Wilson Reading Program; and these had been largely successful… in helping him to decode words, but not in inspiring or helping him to become a motivated, proficient reader. I remember reading a baseball story with Marvin. I was asking him inference-level questions about things that were implied but not directly stated in the text. He became angry and said, "I am telling you what the story says. It's not fair of you to ask me what it doesn't say!" Marvin did not understand that he was supposed to bring his own knowledge of baseball to the reading act so he could create a story world and a visual image of the field, the ballplayers, and the action. When we finished the book, I asked him what the story meant to him personally, and what the author might have been communicating about the ballplayers' actions. He was totally stumped.

"What do you mean, what does it mean? It's a story. Some stuff happened." When I asked him what the most important events were, he told me that he couldn't remember. When I asked him what he had seen when he read the story, he muttered, "See? Words, man, I see nothing but words!"

I asked him to recall the point at which the story had stopped making sense. I'll never forget how sad he looked when he said, "Reading is supposed to make sense? Reading… school… it's never made any sense to me. No sense at all."

Marvin's critique of school and school reading could be interpreted on several levels, but it's clear that school had not helped him to think about reading as a meaning-making pursuit and had never helped him to view reading as a worthwhile activity. He was not aware of how to make meaning when meaning might be breaking down, or what to do about it when it did. He could decode most words and thought that was reading. No wonder he so often insisted that "Reading is *stupid!*"

Parents and schools often collude to promote misconception about reading. I've had parents insist that their child could read or was a good reader because he could decode and identify words. They didn't understand that reading is so much more than that. "I don't know what the trouble is," they'd insist. Schools collude because we often teach reading, particularly with older remedial students like Marvin, by concentrating solely on word-decoding skills. These skills are very important, to be sure, but reading is an integrated process of many word-, sentence-, and text-level strategies. These local-level decoding strategies must be contextualized as only a part and as a means to the end of pursuing larger meanings. This kind of meaning-construction involves a variety of cognitive, emotional, personal, and social processes. Think-alouds, as I hope has been obvious thus far in this book, can highlight the many integrated features of engaged reading.

In this chapter, we'll look at ways to use think-alouds to give students strategies for monitoring comprehension and for "fixing up" their comprehension when it derails. It is absolutely essential to good reading that the reader knows when meaning breaks down and what to do about it. To do this, readers must learn to identify when problems occur, isolate the problem, name the source of confusion, and know how to use strategies to attack and overcome the confusion. This is far from a simple process, and think-alouds can be a powerful way to help.

Think-Alouds Can Target Common Troubles of Struggling Readers

- *Poor readers often plow right through a reading, decoding words but not comprehending the text.* Think-alouds can help because they require the reader to slow down and to reflect on how they are understanding and interpreting text.

- *Poor readers don't bring meaning forward with them, building it as they work through a text.* Think-alouds can help students to identify, consolidate, and summarize the growing meanings they make while reading so that the meaning can be used.

- *Poor readers just give up.* Think-alouds can help by giving students strategies to try in lieu of giving up.

I'm indebted to the work of James Baumann and his colleagues in using think-alouds for monitoring comprehension. Their studies, among others, have shown that think-alouds are a highly effective way to help students deal with the monitoring and repair of comprehension difficulties. (See especially Baumann, 1986, 1992, 1993.)

CONSIDER THIS

As is true for any techniques for assisting kids' performance, the think-aloud is a means to an end and not the end in itself. Once students have mastered the strategies of monitoring their reading to improve comprehension, you will not need to do think-alouds to assist them with this. Or, if students use some strategies but not others, think-alouds should be designed and cued to focus what students do not yet know.

From Modeling to Students' Independent Use: Basic Steps

TEACHER DOES/STUDENTS WATCH

To introduce my students to the notion of checking understanding while reading, I model a wide variety of fix-up strategies, help students identify them, and then post a list or flow chart of them in the classroom (see the following example). I tell the students that the strategies outlined here will help them monitor their comprehension and read better, no matter what they are reading.

TEACHER DOES/STUDENTS HELP

Then I read another text and ask students to help me go through the process we have outlined by prompting me and explaining the steps I should try.

STUDENTS DO/TEACHER HELPS

When the process of comprehension monitoring becomes relatively clear to them, students then take over the process themselves in small groups, and when ready, of course, begin to use the process on their own.

Tips for Guiding Students

- I start off telling students to continually pause and ask themselves the question: Does this make sense?
- I tell kids who answer "no, this isn't making sense" to use the most basic fix-up strategies of 1) rereading, 2) reading ahead, 3) skipping or filling in a word. I later introduce other strategies, some of which need to be modeled and taught more explicitly.

Remember that any time you introduce a strategy and kids don't or can't use it, you must go back and do more modeling and provide more assistance. On the other hand, if kids quickly take to the strategy, let them take more responsibility for it, and move on to teach something else with which they are having more difficulty.

FLOW CHART OF COMPREHENSION-MONITORING BEHAVIORS

1 Read a passage of text.

2 Pause, ask yourself: Does this make sense? (Do this periodically; pause at ends of natural text segments like paragraphs.)
- Option, check yourself: Can I retell the important points of the last segment? Other options: Can I say it in my own words? Are my hypotheses holding up, or do I need to change my predictions?

3 If Yes, reading makes sense! Continue reading (back to #1). If No, continue to #4.

4 Ask: When did I lose track? When did it start to go wrong?

5 Isolate cause of difficulty **(each difficulty is matched to an appropriate problem-solving strategy in #6).** Did I:
a. run into difficulty with a word or words? (vocabulary)
b. stop concentrating?
c. read it too fast?
d. lose the thread of meaning? i.e., struggle to understand how it relates to what was written before?
e. not know enough about the topic that's been taken up?
f. lose image or mental representation? i.e., Can't "see" what it is I am reading about?
g. not understand how text is organized and where it is headed, what I should expect?
h. try a strategy that didn't work? Not know which strategy to try?

6 Use an appropriate strategy for your problem.

    a. Skip the word and read to end of sentence or segment, trying to figure it out from the context.

a. Guess the meaning or substitute a word that seems to fit and see if it makes sense.

a. Ask someone the meaning of the word, look for definition in text, look up in dictionary.

b. Reread the segment.

b. Read aloud—it can really help to hear the text. Or ask someone else to read it aloud to you.

c. Slow down and reread, or read aloud.

d. Chunk the confusing segment with what came before or what comes afterward. Try to understand a whole chunk that is short and manageable.

e. Identify the topic and bring personal knowledge to bear. What do you know about this or a similar topic that might help you?

e. Find out more about the topic—read something else that is simpler or more introductory; use a reference book; ask someone else who knows more.

f. Try to create an image or mind picture of what is going on (could use picture mapping, tableaux, or mapping techniques from next chapter).

g. Ask: How is the text organized? How should what comes before help me with my problem? (Very helpful to know that in an argument a claim is followed by evidence and evidence is usually followed by a warrant; in cause and effect text structures, causes are followed by effects; in classification, one class or category is followed by a parallel category, etc. See Chapter 6.)

g. Recognize and use text features and cues to text structure like transitions, headings, illustrations, and captions, charts, etc.

g. Ask: Am I supposed to make an inference? Fill a gap in the story? Put several pieces of information together to see a pattern?

h. Read on and see if the confusion clears up.

h. If still confused, try another strategy or ask for help. Ask a peer, then the teacher or another expert reader.

7 Check understanding—if Yes, back to #1 to continue reading; if No, ask for help.

 ## STUDENTS DO/TEACHER HELPS

THE STOP, FIX, ASK CHECKLIST

When students are ready to take over the process of self-monitoring in small groups or individually, I might give them a Stop, Fix, and Ask Checklist (see next page). This checklist is an expansion and adaptation of the Stop-Think Strategy of Sue Mowery which I discovered on the Internet.

Name _____ Date _____

Stop, Ask, Fix: Student Checklist

Give yourself a short self-assessment. Read through the following list and put a check mark next to the strategies you regularly use to read a difficult book or piece of writing. Which ones don't you use? These should be strategies to keep in mind the next time you read something challenging. Keep this checklist at your side as you read a text. Use it to help prompt you to use the appropriate strategies available for watching and fixing your comprehension.

ASK, When reading a difficult text...

❏ I periodically stop and ask, "Does this make sense?"

❏ I express the difference between my own knowledge and beliefs and ideas expressed in text.

❏ I express awareness or lack of awareness of what the content means.

❏ I express doubt about understanding when I am unsure or when meaning is unclear.

❏ I ask "Where did I lose track?"

❏ I identify the place where I began to lose comprehension.

❏ I use fix-up strategies when I experience problems.

❏ I reread.

❏ I read on and try to clear up the confusion.

❏ I substitute words I know (and that fit the context) to replace words I don't understand to see if that works.

❏ I make mind pictures to "see" in my head what the text means.

❏ I connect what I am reading to what I have read previously in this text, and what I have read and knew before I read this text. I may ask an author-and-me question because my personal knowledge may help me figure out the meaning.

❏ I ask myself questions (Why did the character do this? Why did the author put this in? How is this important? Am I supposed to "think and search" or infer?).

❏ I use these other strategies: [WOL]

❏ I ask for help if I have made attempts to understand but can't get it. I ask a peer and then I ask my teacher or another adult.

This is an expansion and adaptation of the Stop-Think Strategy of Sue Mowery.

Improving Comprehension with Think-Aloud Strategies • Scholastic Professional Books

Let Students Know It's Okay to Ask for Assistance

Let your students know that *readers should ask for help.* It's so crucial that we dispel the myth that prevails among students that "smart" readers don't ever hit an obstacle in their reading or ask for assistance. In my various studies involving at-risk boys, I found that they were so eager to appear competent that they would avoid asking for help at all

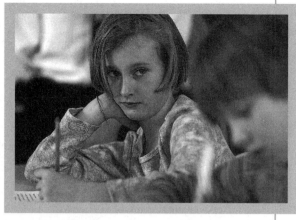

Encourage your students to ask for help. This is a strategy good readers use all the time!

costs. They would rather say, like Marvin, that "reading is stupid" than lay themselves open to the charge that they might be stupid, slow, or anything less than totally competent. (Is this a variation on men's unwillingness to ask for directions when they are lost?)

I make asking for help part of the way we do things—and giving help part of our classroom responsibility. I model asking for a hand with many things in the classroom. I share lots of stories about how my adult book club members help each other understand difficult passages, concepts, and books. I tell them how I e-mail and call friends when I don't understand data I am collecting, or an article I am reading. I tell them that with a doctorate in reading, I still have trouble reading many things. I stress that what makes me an expert is that I know when, how, and who to ask for help.

TEACHER DOES/STUDENTS WATCH

REVEAL YOUR MONITORING PROCESS (INCLUDING YOUR MISSTEPS!)

I often like to read aloud a short segment of a text I haven't read before, and one I suspect will be challenging for me. It's often from a current issue of a magazine I subscribe to, such as *American Heritage, The Atlantic Monthly,* or *Popular Mechanics.* (This models wide reading interests and brings a variety of texts that might interest students into the classroom.) The selected article must be culturally interesting to the kids, but not too esoteric.

By reading a text "cold," students can see that I struggle with new texts too. Rabinowitz and Smith argue that teachers usually "read against reading" by teaching texts they have read multiple times. Students end up with the false impression that reading, comprehending, and having insights about a text is effortless for the teacher and thus feel that they will never be good readers, because they could never read with the facility the teacher displays (Rabinowitz and Smith, 1998). (True enough. I have read *Macbeth* at least sixty times. I've read *Roll of Thunder, Hear My Cry* at least thirty times. My students cannot hope to read these texts as I do or understand them the way I do.) Demonstrating your own struggles and fix-up strategies is a great antidote to this problem.

I always start by setting a purpose and showing how this purpose fits some kind of inquiry I am interested in. As I often as I can, I select a text that relates to our in-class inquiry projects or unit or some other issue that the kids are involved in; this is a great way to show them that the issues we are taking up in our class are issues out in the world and that other people are thinking, arguing, researching, writing, and conversing about them. It is also a great way to show them the variety of journals, magazines, informational texts, electronic resources, and Web sites that are available to them.

Recently, I brought in an article from *Modern Maturity* ("Male Bonding," Jan./Feb. 2000, pp. 52–57) about the appeal of James Bond. The article fit our current unit on relationships, since we could use the romantic relationships of James Bond as a topic we could explore and critique as part of our inquiry. (Plus, the class knew that I was engaged in a study, using several of them as informants, in which I was exploring how males construct their male identities.)

To open the think-aloud, I preview, activate my background, and set purposes:

> *I'm reading this because I am interested in how men construct their identities and act them out. I'm hoping this article can help me. Also we're studying good relationships in this class, and I wonder if we'll think that Bond's professional and personal relationships are the kinds we would call "good." I know a lot about James Bond. I've seen plenty of the movies. I like them and for some reason I'm embarrassed about that … I wonder why. They start in the most action-packed way, there is incredible danger, Bond always escapes from an inescapable near-death situation. There are always beautiful women… maybe that is why I am embarrassed… I'm like a little boy hooked on women's outward appearances and violent action. I do wonder why I like Bond. Maybe there is some deep reason that has to do with being a man in this culture. Maybe this article can explain that. There've been several characters who have played the part of Bond. Sean Connery was the first and I liked him the best. Hmmm. Check out the title. The title is interesting.*

TEXT	THINK-ALOUD
Male Bonding	**Hmm. I wonder why this title? Is it just a play on words—you know James "Bond" and "bonding," or is the author going to suggest that men bond or identify with James Bond in some way? And look at all the pictures—Bond with beautiful women and engaged in death-defying stunts.... Is there the suggestion that this is what being a man is all about? Does this explain extreme sports?**
The obvious place to start, if you want to understand the continuing appeal of James Bond,	**Oh, good ... I do want to understand this and I hope it will help me understand how men think about being men.**
is with the nature of hero-ism. Bond, like all other heroes, is a projection of wish fulfillment, especial-ly the will to power.	**I don't get it. I'll reread ... wish fulfillment ... maybe like a childish desire about something that I just have to have...**
Though we in the audi-ence are circumscribed by our personal limitations,	**What does "circumscribed" mean? What if I replace it with "imprisoned"? Yes, that makes sense.**
Bond has the talent and temerity to do exactly as he pleases—not to men-tion the license to kill...	**Hmm, is this making sense? I'll retell to see.... So this means that Bond can do whatever he wants. I'd like to do whatever I want, but I can't, so I like to identify with him? It's a hypothesis anyway. I'll see if the rest of the arti-cle bears that out. If this is true, then no won-der I'm embarrassed—liking Bond is showing what a kid I really am, only wanting my own way! I wonder if I can agree with that. Being that way certainly wouldn't lead to a good rela-tionship. It reminds me of the poem we just read, Shel Silverstein's "My Way."**

With this think-aloud, I was able to model how purpose-setting guides reading, how to use self-questioning, word replacement, rereading, and the intention to read on to verify hypotheses, the use of background knowledge and personal connections to build meaning, and retelling. I might use such a think-aloud after students have been introduced to monitoring since it shows how many different fix-up techniques should be used and integrated while reading, or I might use it as a review and have kids identify the techniques I am using (Teacher Does/Students Help).

When I did this one, I told kids that if I had had too much trouble, I would not have hesitated to ask them or others for help, and I even told them how I irritate my wife by interrupting her reading in bed to ask her questions about what I am reading!

It is very worthwhile to do this kind of "cold read" for your students. Kids get to see the strategies in action, used for real purposes, and can extrapolate from your modeling how they can give them a try, too. Seeing a teacher wrestle with a new text is priceless: they discover that difficulty does not deter or embarrass you; you have ways of dealing with the problems you encounter.

 ## TEACHER DOES/STUDENTS HELP

Sharing Strategies

After modeling with a few different texts, I read aloud to the students as they read along. I ask them to pause when I do and be ready to voice what they are doing to monitor their understanding. We then identify the monitoring strategies they've used and what other strategies they could call on. (The "Teacher Does/Students help" phase; as I let them take over more of the responsibility, this becomes the "Students Do/Teacher Helps" phase.)

One day, during an integrated science-language arts unit on "Hidden Realities" I read to students from *MicroAliens: Dazzling Journeys with an Electron Microscope*. We were reading a section about microorganisms in the typical house, things like fungi, bacteria, mites, fibers, and fleas found in clothes, ventilation systems, furniture, and even our food. The kids were all acting disgusted (of course), which showed their engagement, when I paused and asked how they were monitoring their comprehension.

Pam: "I'm asking right now: 'Does this make sense?' Just like you taught us! [Laughter. I say: "Very Good, Pam!"] It does make sense and I can put it in my own words [Pam gives a quick summary of the last segment] and I'm asking how much worse will the next chapter be when they describe the outdoors!? Maybe Joe's house will look good by comparison!"

JW: Ha! OK, class, what techniques did she use?

[The student identified the "Does it make sense?" question and the retelling as a meaning-making technique, and the hypothesizing/predicting to lead her reading on.]

Sam: "I didn't get the paragraph about Bacillus mega—I can't say that word ["Bacterium," another student calls out]. Thank you. Thank you. It says they 'excrete' valuable chemicals into the soil. I think I know what 'excrete' means but I'm not sure. When I replace it with the word I know I'm not sure it makes sense. I mean, can bacteria do that stuff? [Kids laugh.]

JW: "They sure can, and it fertilizes the ground. By the way, Sam, thanks for your restraint! OK, blue collar scholars, what techniques did Sam just use?"

[The students identified word replacement and rereading strategies and asking for help as strategies Sam used.]

Now the students were ready to proceed to working in small groups or pairs (Students Do/Teacher Observes or Helps), and later to individual work (Student Does/Teacher Observes and Assesses). As they did so, they used the monitoring check sheets, as needed, (see pages 100, 120 and 170), but also a variety of coding and underlining techniques, desribed below.

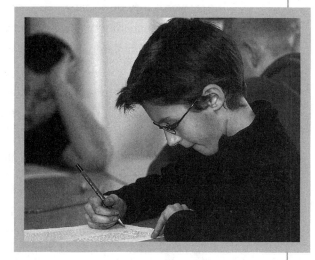

Self-monitoring strategies help students to continue engaging with texts even the material is challenging.

 ## STUDENTS DO/TEACHER OBSERVES

Underlining and Coding to Monitor Comprehension

Inspired by John Ciardi's colored-chalk approach to analyzing poetry, a group of my student teachers adapted this technique for use with think-alouds. The basic idea, which I've also seen used widely in the National Writing Project (I learned it from Tom Fox of the Northern California Writing Project), is for students to use colored pencils, markers, and various color "codes" to record how they are comprehending various passages of the text. My student teachers gave the technique a few new, effective twists:

Checking Comprehension: Ask students to put a check mark in the margin of a text after each paragraph.
- ✓ means they understand.
- ✓+ means they really understand it and are really interested in it.
- ✓- means they do not understand and that they need to go back and use a fix-it strategy with that paragraph.

Circles, Squiggles, and Bold: In this variation, students:
__ circle words they don't know ("lassoing them" so that they are kept in mind to fix).
__ use squiggly underlining to signal confusion (i.e., meaning is wavy and ambiguous).
__ use bold underlining for key details (bold assertion that you are sure this is important).

Color Notes: Students use colored pencils or markers to:
__ underline in green (a positive, cool, let's-keep-trucking color!) if they are getting it.
__ underline in yellow (slow down! uncertainty) if they are becoming confused.
__ underline in red if they are lost (red meaning danger!). Students also record the fix-up strategies they used—or ought to use—in the margins near the red underlining.

Of course, many other variations of this kind of monitoring marking can be used! Teachers and students will invariably come up with their own color codes, and these can be made to fit the particular needs of the moment.

Smooth Sailing: Navigating Trouble Spots for Peers

One of the best ways to get kids to synthesize and practice what they've learned about monitoring comprehension is this: I have small groups of students pick out articles that interest them and that they know something about from the day's newspaper (or a current magazine, Web site, etc.). I give them about five to ten minutes (depending on the article's length) to analyze the piece so they can give advice to classmates who don't know about the topic or who haven't dealt with that kind of text. Students have to identify the potential problems a more "novice" reader might encounter, and the monitoring strategies that could be used to overcome these challenges. In doing this, you cast the kids as "experts" to see how they can help other readers approach both the *what* (declarative knowledge) and the *how* (procedural knowledge for reading this kind of text).

One group of boys gravitated to a story about the previous night's NCAA basketball championship. They really wanted to read about the game, but with that done, they began to analyze the article for trouble spots.

TEXT	THINK-ALOUD
Spartans too strong for Florida; Michigan State Wins title By Jim O'Connell, The Associated Press	**The title doesn't really tell people who don't know what this is about. They won't know who the Spartans are or that the title refers to the NCAA basketball championship game. They'll need some help.** *[Notice that the students understand the importance of the title for orienting the reader to the text. They also understand that this title requires some inferring that readers not experienced with the topic may not be able to make.]*
Indianapolis—This time there was no Magic, just Mateen.	**People who don't know about basketball won't know about Magic Johnson, the NBA all-star, or about Mateen Cleaves. Plus why should they care? This article would need frontloading for them to get it!** *[Notice that the students clearly understand the importance of bringing personal knowledge and purposes to bear and how to help the reader with this.]*
Michigan State, with Magic Johnson cheering in the stands, won its second national championship as Mateen Cleaves led the Spartans to an 89–76 victory over Florida on Monday night.	**Will they know what it is the championship of, and why they should care? You know, even we don't care—it was a horrible year for NCAA basketball— the tournament really sucked after the third round. All the best teams were knocked out and the Spartans had an easy run. SYRACUSE FOREVER!** *[Notice how the students highlight the importance of purposeful reading. Then they can't help making a judgment of their own!]*

It was 21 years ago that the championship game between Michigan State and Indiana State—Magic vs. Bird—changed the landscape of college basketball.

Why did it change the landscape and what does landscape mean here? Why is this important? The reader should get more help here from the author. *[Here they are concerned about vocabulary and helping the reader use it to negotiate meaning.]*

The article and their commentary continued for another several paragraphs.

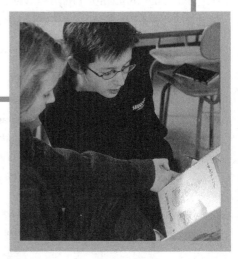

Fiona and Jasmine study a picture book they plan to read with second graders. They anticipate difficulties the younger students may experience.

Activities such as this engage students in thinking about how text structures work to prompt particular kinds of readerly activity. This can only help to enhance students' own reading and their own writing of more friendly and communicative texts (for more on reading various genres and text structures, see Chapter 6).

 ## TEACHER DOES/STUDENTS MUST HELP!

An Extreme Sport: Watch the Teacher Sweat!

I have students bring in a text that they think will confound me. We choose a short section, usually from the beginning of the text but not always. (Choosing a section from the middle or end of a text poses more challenges for figuring out what it's about.) I encourage students to bring in a text they know well or that's about something they know about. This makes them the expert and me the novice.

Students enjoy trying to stump me and enjoy watching me sweat! This is good. It shows them that I struggle too and that I know what strategies to use, even if I am reduced to asking them to help me out—which I usually do have to do!!

Students often bring in technical manuals, something from their parents' workplace, or popular-culture texts and song lyrics. I am quick to point out to them that many texts are written for particular audiences and that I may not belong to the audience. I also point out features of texts that are not reader-friendly. This is not to make excuses but to bring to their attention that faltering comprehension is sometimes not the fault of the reader alone. I emphasize that they must think about their audience and write reader-friendly prose, no matter what they write. I also highlight that even when authors and texts do not provide all the help they need to, readers still have ways to understand things that are unclear.

When students watch their teacher navigate a challenging text, it demonstrates to them that even expert readers experience difficulty, and that they tap into a wide repertoire of strategies for addressing difficulties.

An example is Stetsasonic's rap song "Talkin' All That Jazz," which some students brought to me. I understood the words literally, and I recognized the genre of the song as an argument—in fact, the first stanza sets up a kind of verbal confrontation. But I didn't get what the argument was about. I isolated my problem in the lines: "Talkin' 'bout Rap/Sayin' all that crap/About how we sample." My students had a good laugh about my lack of knowledge as they explained "sampling" as a "convention" (yes, one student used that term, which showed he'd been paying attention to our work on text-specific task expectations and the coding of particular genres!) of rap songs, in which the rappers use lines from other famous songs, or even blend in recordings of previous songs, speeches, and popular-culture texts into their song. I used this exchange to highlight the importance of background knowledge to reading and the fact that texts are written for particular audiences with a specific knowledge base.

Later in the song I read: "Think Rap is a fad, you must be mad/'Cause we're so bad, we get respect you never had/Tell the truth, James Brown was old/Till Eric and Rak came out with "I Got Soul"/Rap brings back old R&B and if we would not/People could have forgot…"

Again I isolated my problem as the line with Eric and Rak. My students told me they were a new group that "sampled" James Brown. Suddenly I understood the argument of the song and tried it out with my students: rappers use sampling to "bring forward" the history of their people and their art. In fact, I remembered and mentioned to them that many African American authors and artists use a technique called "voice blending" of prior voices with a new text. Martin Luther King Jr. and James Weldon Johnson made extensive use of this technique and it is culturally valued.

My students concurred with my summary, and we later read some sermons and speeches of these ministers and looked at the sources they used so we could compare voice blending to sampling.

GETTING IT RIGHT BY GETTING RIGHTED!

I just returned from a brief break from revising of this book, during which time I went whitewater kayaking with two of my friends. The water on the Soudabscook Stream was as high as I have ever seen it. The whitewater coursed and choked down the narrow creek and swamped up over the banks.

When I first saw this scene I was ready to climb back in the car. I have kayaked this stream before but it had never looked like this. At flood stage, it gave me a new challenge, one I wasn't sure I was up for.

To psych myself up, I remembered that I had several kayaking self-correction strategies. I knew how to eddy out to catch a rest and scout the river. I knew how to brace with my paddle to keep from going over. But if I rolled or was knocked over, I knew how to Eskimo roll to right myself. If I got caught on the wrong side of the river, I knew how to ferry across for a better approach...

Thus fortified, I headed downstream. It was a scary ride and I used every self-correction technique I knew. When the run was completed, I was pretty darn proud of myself. I'd approached a more challenging task than I ever had before. I had been in several tough situations—I'd even gotten caught in a "strainer," a tree submerged in the water—but with my fix-up strategies and the help of my partners, I was able to get downriver safely and had an absolutely thrilling time. Without the fix-up strategies the scene would have been grim!

This is what fix-up strategies do for any practitioner of any craft, including reading. With fix-up strategies, kids will have the confidence to undertake new challenges. And with the help of such strategies, they can comprehend and reach new reading achievements. That can and should be a real thrill for both teacher and student.

CHAPTER 5

INTENSIFIED INVOLVEMENT:
Getting Visual, Emotional, and Verbal with Texts

Students rehearse for a drama activity based on a
novel they have just read. The activity is helping
them to "think-aloud" as characters.

Now it's time to use think-alouds to increase students' engagement with the text—to hone their ability to get totally wrapped up in the prose and to reread and reflect on their reading in ways that deepen understanding. Just as there are strategies readers use to get into a story or to check their understanding, there are certain "moves" readers make to intensify their textual involvement, their enjoyment and understanding of texts. Three major ways of promoting engagement are to improve the ways we see or visualize a text, to improve the way we engage emotionally with it, and to improve the way that we converse with authors and "talk back" to them about their work and the ideas expressed there. These are the strategy "families" we will concern ourselves with in this chapter.

Engaged Reading

I can't remember not loving to read. I can't remember not being involved in a book. When I finish a novel, it seems as though there are always others I've started or wanted to start, waiting in the wings. One day I'm reading *Cold Mountain,* and making my way toward that place in the Blue Ridge with Inman, doing my best to avoid the Home Guard and find my way back to my love and my home. The next day I'm sailing the high seas with Jack Aubrey and Stephen Maturin of Patrick O'Brian's seagoing sagas. It's a family joke that I won't speak to anyone or pack lunches until I've read the morning newspaper. Magazines, biographies, volumes of poetry, and coffee table books strew my office and home. The Internet beckons with Web sites galore of great interest. For me, a day without reading would be like a day without eating. I recognize my own voracious appetite for reading in some of my students. But I recognize it in far too few of them.

My reading life is filled with intensity. Just this morning I was reading Paul Hawken's *The Ecology of Commerce.* I could see in my mind the chemical companies pouring their waste into rivers. I knew that dioxin and the other chemicals they spew into the air and water do not degrade and will threaten human life for thousands of years. I argued with myself about why the environment has been lost as a theme for our presidential election. I became so angry about how we ignore all the evidence that we are destroying our environment that I had to stop reading. I announced, "I can't read any more of this right now." My kids, who are used to my talking aloud, looked up. Fiona asked, "What's eating you, Pappy?" But they could see from my deep breathing and distracted look that I couldn't answer right then so they returned to their own reading.

When I read a story, I feel as though I am *in* that story world. Sometimes I am a character, sometimes I accompany the characters and act on their behalf—or try to. I intensely visualize characters, settings, situations, and events—so much so that I can describe places and activities that are not described, or are only hinted at, in the text itself. I often take issue with the author (especially when reading informational texts) about the way she wrote something or about the message she is trying to convey. Sometimes I actively agree or argue with her, talking back to her as I read her work, "You go, girl!" or "You gotta be kidding me!"

I know from my studies of highly engaged adolescent readers that I am not unique. Expert student readers, even at the upper elementary and middle school levels, do all of these same things. Poorer readers often do none of them. The relationship between engagement and reading achievement is at least correlative and perhaps causative.

I've found think-alouds to be one way to encourage less engaged readers to recognize and take on the attitudes and strategies that will open themselves to the intense participation and visualization involved in the best reading of stories, arguments, descriptions, and other kinds of texts. When students engage in this kind of intense experience, they begin to see why some people love reading. A whole new world of experience is opened to them. Motivation awakens, and a door of possibility opens.

Visual Think-Alouds

Though I am aware of various kinds of visual response in the research literature, I happened to get the idea for visual think-alouds, like so many of my best teaching ideas, from my students. When I was pursuing my research on engaged and unengaged reading for *You Gotta BE the Book,* I was finding out all kinds of things about how readers enter into stories and arguments: by activating prior knowledge and knowledge of the genre, by expressing high expectations of benefiting from the text, of being enlightened or entertained, and much more. But above all, my engaged readers were quickly immersed in the text by intensely participating and visualizing and elaborating on the textual details.

One characteristic that showed up in all engaged reading was that it was a highly visual experience. As engaged readers participated in and visualized texts, without any prompting, they brought their own lives to the reading; projected themselves into the

Students composing visual think-
alouds of their reading.

textual world; judged characters; expressed predictions and expectations; role-played and enacted scenes in their minds and even sometimes physically; referred to authors and characters as friends or acquaintances that they cared about; visualized and inferred physical features, mental images with emotional power for them, scenes and events—and much more. As they did so, they called upon a wide variety of mental and emotional processes to awaken these imaginative, intuitive responses.

My data demonstrated that if students did not visualize and participate in a textual world, they were then unable to do all of the other kinds of things expert readers often do with text during or after their reading and that students are sometimes asked to do in school. For instance, they are asked to reflect on their reading to consider its meaning and how that meaning was constructed and communicated through the text; to isolate and appreciate the use of writerly conventions; to bring what they had read back to their lives to apply it. Most of my students did not visualize or participate in story worlds in any way. I realized that my students were continually asked to reflect on experiences they had never had and that no one had ever helped them to have! No wonder they were so often unsuccessful and frustrated!

So I began experimenting with all kinds of interventions to support kids' visualization while they read—picture mapping, tableaux, mind movies, symbolic story representation, museum exhibits, a variety of drama-in-education strategies, and so on. (All will be explained in later books in this series.) One day, while doing a think-aloud, a student asked, "Why can't we do drawings on our think-alouds, instead of writing?"

What?

"A visual think-aloud, kind of like…" another student continued.

"Brilliant!" I replied.

"Really?" they said, not quite so sure.

Since then, I often encourage students to use drawings when doing a think-aloud. When I offer this option, well over half include drawings of some kind. Some students, typically those labeled as LD, do their entire think-aloud, or almost all of it, in pictures. As I've argued in previous books, most of these students are certainly not "learning disabled." They are instead "differently abled," in ways that are not typically valued by school. Many of my LD students are very visual, and when they do think-alouds that build on this strong suit, they begin to flourish.

Visual think-alouds, and the other techniques offered in this chapter, promote ways of reading not often fostered in school. When students are helped to visualize and participate in textual worlds in new ways, engagement is intensified and comprehension is improved.

STARGAZING

I was reading *Number the Stars,* the Newbery Medal–winning book by Lois Lowry, with a group of sixth graders. This book is set in Denmark during World War II. Annemarie's family, like many Danes, risked their own lives to protect their Jewish neighbors from the Nazi invaders. Annemarie's family, in fact, helped their friends the Rosens, including Annemarie's best friend Ellen, to escape to safety in Sweden. In the final chapter, the war is ending, and Annemarie's family anticipates the Rosens' return.

I asked my students to engage in a visual think-aloud of this final chapter. I asked them to read the ending and to write or draw their visual and sensory engagement with the story's conclusion. I emphasized that this was a strategy that would make them better

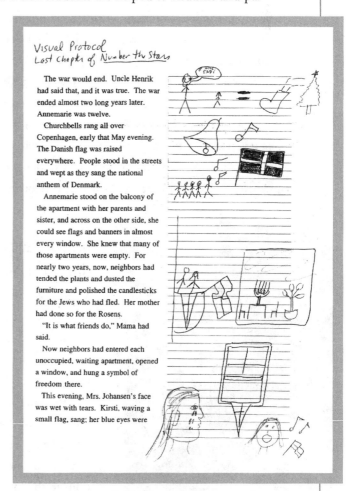

A student's visual protocol of the last chapter of *Number the Stars* by Lois Lowry. The student uses icons to visualize what is described, indexical pictures to explore meaning, and symbols to make connections to her personal life.

readers and that it wasn't meant to be an art project.

Some students drew what I would call *iconic* pictures or rough estimations of the literal surface meaning: for instance, stick figures in Copenhagen's square waving flags or a stick-figure firing squad shooting Peter Nielsen. A few students did more elaborate, realistic sketches.

Others drew *indexical* pictures, images that represented a part of something bigger or suggested something related; for example, drawing a flag or a ringing church bell to signify patriotic celebration, a teardrop falling from an eye to suggest relief and an overwhelming emotion, a gravestone to indicate Peter's execution, a menorah on an empty table to signify the Rosen's empty but maintained apartment. Other pictures were *symbolic* and got at a deeper meaning; for instance the use of a peace sign with an exclamation mark to show that peace had come to the country quite suddenly.

All of these drawings helped the students to "see" and share the story world, to experience it on the levels of action and surface meaning. Other kinds of drawings, like the symbolic or indexical ones, helped students to reflect on how the text was constructed, what it meant, and how it affected them.

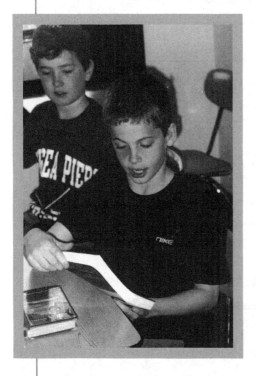

Giving Visual Thinking a Voice: Discussing Students' Images

Like most of the think-alouds we do, I always ask students to share their visual think-alouds with each other and to talk about why they drew the pictures the way they did, what the drawings mean, and what they learned about the text and their reading from drawing and thinking about them. The drawings always reveal more about a reader's thinking and response than is immediately obvious. Also, the pictures are objects to think with, and talking about them brings new realizations to the forefront. Neo-Vygotskians believe that learning floats on a sea of talk and that we must get students to talk through their content understandings and thinking processes. Visual think-alouds are great because the students have something they have made to talk about and think with.

For example, while completing a think-aloud of the last chapter of *Number the Stars*, Julieanne drew Annemarie's opened blue trunk, inside of which was a faded yellow dress topped by Ellen's broken necklace chain and Star of David. Though this appeared to be simply an iconic rendition of concrete description from the text, this student explained her picture symbolically to her reading group:

> *Drawing this made me see that the people had to hide themselves and who they were to survive. And even though this is a happy day and they can come out of hiding—this is why Annemarie opens the trunk—the trunk is blue for sadness, but the dress is yellow for happy times… The dress, which is like the happy times and celebrations, is faded and worn… it stands for them and their state of mind… They are happy but they are damaged too and I have to ask if they will ever be as happy as they were before… And Ellen's connections to others, which is the necklace, is broken. It can be fixed, like Papa says, but it won't be the same. This all shows that even though they protected what they loved, the war still damaged their lives and their lives will never be the same. But the Star of David still gleams gold … so her faith and her Jewishness are strong as ever, which is a really good sign! So I felt the great happiness of the characters and their relief, I felt glad that they still had faith, but I also felt sad to remember the people who were killed, and the suffering, which will never be forgotten. The war will always be with them.*

The last drawing of her think-aloud was a two-faced figure smiling on one side and crying on the other: "This is me… totally happy and totally sad at the same time. Not confused, but both at the same time as I read the end of the book."

Though I had read the book several times, I had never seen the trunk and its contents as a symbol. This student told me that drawing during the think-aloud had helped her "to notice the trunk." "I knew it was important, and as I drew it, I understood what the author wanted me to make of it," she said.

Julieanne's incisive reading was an exception rather than a rule. Nevertheless, she was able to use the think-aloud to share her way of reading symbolic details with the rest of the class. This in turn makes her strategies visible and available to other students, who (in this case and many others I've observed) were very eager to borrow and use a more expert reader's techniques. It also gave us the opportunity to talk about symbolism and strategies used to notice and interpret a symbol. Julieanne told us that the trunk and necklace "got a lot of attention" and they "were the last objects described in the book, so I knew the author wanted me to notice them." Julieanne knew that "colors are a tip-off" too, and can be interpreted symbolically, and so are "objects people care about or use a lot, like the Star of David… or the necklace, which is a circle, and shapes can be important too!"

When she discussed the symbolism of color, someone asked whether the Swedish flag was yellow and blue. After ascertaining that this was the case, this student maintained that the trunk was symbolic of Sweden, where Ellen's family went into hiding. From this discussion we were able to put together a *heuristic,* or problem-solving guide, for reading symbolism.

THE PROCESS OF READING SYMBOLISM: STEPS TO TAKE

1 Recognize action or object as symbolic
Rules of notice to watch for as you read:

- If an object has obvious symbolic meanings, pay attention! (For example, a menorah symbolizes Jewishness, a cross symbolizes Christianity, a flag symbolizes a country or patriotism.)
- If an action is described in detail or seems to you to be symbolic, pay attention! (For example, if an author devotes a paragraph at the opening of a chapter to describing a wishing well outside the main character's home, he probably intends it as symbolic; references to flying often means a desire to get away or escape; names of characters and places are often symbolic.)

A familiar object or action may be a symbol if:

- it relates to the title
- it is described in great detail, or with a striking metaphor
- the author uses the object or action in unexpected ways
  - it is given undue attention
  - a character(s) associates the object with someone or something
  - a character(s) interacts with the object
  - it keeps coming up: there is repetition using the object or action
  - characters talk about it or pay attention to it
  - it appears at an important point in

A Reminder: It's a Means to an End

As we've seen, doing think-alouds, and creating class-generated lists like the symbolism one just shown, invite us to calm our reading and responding pace enough that we can notice a book's crucial details and conventions and make meaning of them. It's like that old advice, "stop and smell the flowers." Eventually, readers internalize the ability to do this without slowing down to write down their comments, glance at a list, or draw what they are visualizing. The visual think-aloud has then served its purpose. A new strategic process will have been internalized.

On the next page you'll find a checksheet for students. Have them complete it after they have done a think-aloud to assess how well they have visualized. You could also use it as an informal assessment.

---

the story (in the beginning, at chapter's end, at the climax, the ending)

- it appears as a surprising and inconsistent detail, or at a change in the text
- it uses color, a number, a shape, an animal
- the object or action itself changes in some obvious way, or is used in some new or obvious way

2 Entertain ideas about the object or action's symbolic meaning

For example, if it uses color, a number, a shape—you'll have to consider the cultural significance of the color, number, or shape, e.g., red usually means love, 13 means bad luck, a circle means wholeness and harmony. Some more examples: a mirror might symbolize self-reflection; an object belonging to a deceased relative might symbolize a character's feelings about family or identity; an owl might signify wisdom; an egg fertility, rebirth or perfection.

3 Infer larger meaning and its significance to the story

Now ask yourself, okay, so what does this symbol (of luck, loss, courage, etc.) express about a character? About the story's theme? For example, it's not enough to decide that the green light at the end of the dock in F. Scott Fitzgerald's *The Great Gatsby* is symbolic of Jay Gatsby's social aspirations, you have to infer that it represents the futility and tragedy of Gatsby's quest because he will never attain the status he desires. And perhaps it represents Fitzgerald's own jaded view of society.

Visualization Check Sheet for Readers

Check the moves you typically make or the moves you made in a recent think-aloud.
Provide examples. Which moves do you not make but think you could?
Set a goal to try one or two of these during your next reading.

____ I use sensory images like sounds, physical sensations, smells, touch, and emotions described in the story to help me picture the story.

As I read I create pictures in my mind of:

    ____ events and actions

    ____ characters and their features, clothing, etc.

    ____ settings and situations

____ I create images that elaborate on or embellish story details.

____ I may visualize unmentioned scenes or actions or details, e.g. picturing characters when they were younger or older, seeing a setting in greater detail than it is described, etc.

____ I may visualize myself in the scene.

____ I may imagine meeting a character, having the character enter my daily life.

____ I feel emotions and may visualize in ways that heighten these emotions.

____ I use images and experiences from own life to help me see and experience the text.

Improving Comprehension with Think-Aloud Strategies • Scholastic Professional Books

Conversing with the Author

In the schools where I've taught, we often promote the author as a mythic figure that we bow down before, and we see "uncovering" the author's meaning as the holy grail of interpretation, the be-all and end-all of reading activity.

I've been persuaded by the work of Peter Rabinowitz and Michael Smith (1998) that this kind of interpretation is essential, but that it is the beginning, not the end, of useful conversation

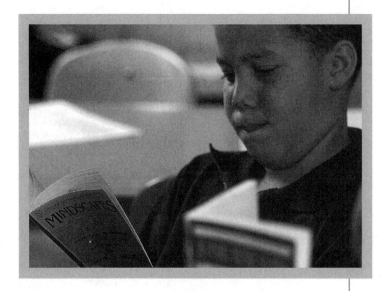

Conversing, agreeing, arguing, and even resisting the visions and ideas of authors is essential to good reading and democratic work, both in and outside the classroom.

and interpretation. Rabinowitz and Smith argue that our first job as readers, just as it is in personal conversation, is to try to understand the author (or speaker) on her own terms. In other words, we read their text (or conversation) the way they want us to read it, by honoring the codes, conventions, and vocabulary that they use, and by trying to understand their text the way it invites us to understand it. Only once we have done this, which is a necessary step to respecting authors (or speakers) and granting them ethical consideration, should we then ask, "How do I feel about that message?" As we do this, we should converse with the author, and accept, adapt, or reject their meaning.

I'm convinced that this kind of conversation, versus passive acceptance of another supposedly superior person's viewpoint, is essential to democracy. My middle school and high school students, particularly my more reluctant or resistant students, find this kind of work fun and satisfying. They have a natural desire to define themselves against or with others. I exploit this tendency by helping them see that authors are not all-knowing gods and that what authors write may not be well constructed, entirely correct, or worthy of their respect. I tell them that it is their job as readers to question, accept, resist, or elaborate upon the author's ideas. Since we do most of our reading as part of inquiry around important themes, my students usually have plenty about which to converse with authors.

Drama: Conversing with the Author

The most immediate and simplest way to introduce the idea of conversing with an author about her ideas and how she wrote and constructed a text is through drama. I usually introduce authorial conversations by playing the role of the author myself (a technique called "teacher in role"). This is a good way to introduce this kind of role-play because I usually know or can find out more about an author than my students. My playing of the author's role also models ways in which it can be done so that students will have an easier time of playing the role of author later on.

My daughter Jasmine, currently in third grade, is in a reading group that is reading the books called *A Series of Unfortunate Events,* by Lemony Snicket. (I am not making this up and the books are hilarious!) The stories revolve around compelling events and issues that almost get resolved… but then get screwed up again at the last moment. The girls in Jasmine's group often groan or yell when such plot twists occur.

Yesterday, they vociferously complained and moaned about the final such twist in Book One, in which the evil Count Olaf, on the verge of being arrested for his treachery, gets away when the theater lights go out. So I asked them: "Why do you think the author wrote the story that way?" and suggested that I become the author so they could ask me.

In drama, students take on other perspectives as they play the parts of authors, characters, ideas or forces that help them to see and understand texts in new ways.

They readily agreed. When they asked why I had let Olaf get away, I answered that I had, after all, warned them. I turned to page 156 and said, "Right here, I warned you, but you wouldn't listen to me! I wrote, and I quote, 'At this point in the story, I feel obliged to interrupt and give you one last warning. As I said at the very beginning, the book you are holding in your hands does not have a happy ending. It may appear now that Count Olaf will got to jail, but it is not so! Etc., etc., etc.!' So why are you blaming me! You decided to read on!”

"You just wrote that because you knew we would have to read to find out what happened!" Jasmine accused.

"And why do you keep warning us like that all through the book?" asked Lauren.

"Because I didn't want to put up with the kind of complaining I am hearing from you now!" I answered. "Besides, it's my book, and I like to be in it every now and then and talk to you all and let you know what you are in for in case you might not want to continue."

"Why couldn't you have let all the children [in the story] have a happy ending!?" Jasmine asked.

"Because he had more books he wanted to write so he couldn't end it," Lauren now accused.

"No, that is not it at all," I disagreed. "I want to make a point to you all about life and the dangers it has and how you overcome them. And it just wouldn't do to simplify it."

The conversation that followed was quite lengthy, involving summaries of various events, predictions about the next book, more accusations hurled at me as the author, and many chances for me to point out how I had written particular scenes, named characters, and intruded with my authorial presence into the text to achieve certain effects.

Hear the Author Speak

This technique, which I learned from Rochelle Ramay of the National Writing Project, works especially well with short texts that have some intensity. When I use it, I often select stories with a first-person narrator.

I have kids go through three steps:

1. I have them underline sections of a text when they see a connection to their own life so they can think-aloud how it connects and why.

2. I have them underline in a different color any section where they think they hear the author speaking to them. (When I introduce this technique, I have students underline the personal connections first and then go back to underline where they hear the author speak. Kids can then explain why these lines felt like the author was speaking directly to them.)

3. I ask them to underline the best lines of the story, in which the author totally nails it. What line speaks for the story or somehow sums up or gets at the central feeling and

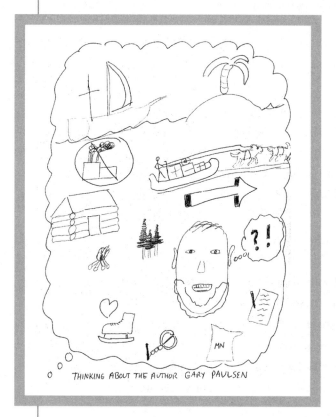

THINKING ABOUT THE AUTHOR GARY PAULSEN

This is a visual picture map of author Gary Paulsen, including ideas from his books and notions about what kind of person he is.

meaning the author was trying to convey? This technique helps kids to talk and write about what they notice and what strikes them as they read. It also helps them to begin considering the author and the text as a construction of that author.

Questioning the Author

An effective strategy for teaching students to do think-aloud-style questioning of the author while reading is QtA, short for "Questioning the Author." This technique is thoroughly explained in an excellent book with the same title, authored by Beck, McKeown, and Hamilton (IRA, 1997).

With a QtA, a reader interacts with a text's ideas to build and deepen understanding. "Our starting point," the authors explain, "is to let students know that the book's content is simply someone's ideas written down, and that this person may not have always expressed things in the clearest or easiest way for readers to understand. Armed with the view of an author as a human being who is potentially fallible, students can view texts as less impersonal, authoritative, and incomprehensible." (see page 18)

This perspective on authors dovetails nicely with Rabinowitz and Smith's view of authorial reading (for more on this, see page 131). For them, both literary and informational texts are constructions of meaning. As constructs, they are always open to interpretation, always arguable, and negotiable. This is just as true with so-called informational texts as it is with literary texts, which admit to being fictions.

To use QtA, you divide a text into short segments. As is true when doing any kind of cued think-aloud, the segments you select should obviously contain information that you can use to model whatever you are spotlighting (inferring, questioning, accessing prior knowledge, use of symbols, and so on).

Beck, et. al. suggest that you use queries—prompts which are designed to assist students to grapple with the author and her ideas, as well as with the way the author has constructed the text. (They differentiate queries from teacher questions, which are generally designed to test literal understanding or start discussion.) These authors provide model queries for both narrative and for informational text. But as a way of transitioning to the informational structures in the next chapter, let's focus on the informational queries here. It's important to note that I have used their queries as models for my own adaptations.

QtA for Informational Texts

Start-Off Queries
(also known as Initiating Queries/Global Queries)

a) Who is the author of this piece? And what do we know about this author?

b) What might be her purpose and agenda in writing this text?

c) What is the author writing about? (What is the general topic or issue?) (see following guide)

d) What important information does the author present? (What are the key details?)

e) What is the author's point? (What is the main idea or central focus? What conclusion do the key details add up to?) What does the author want me to know, think, believe, or do?

Follow-up Queries
(also known as Local-Level Queries)

a) Who is the audience for this piece? (Am I part of this audience? What would I have to know, believe, or be to become part of this audience?)

b) What does the author want this audience to know?

c) What does the author want the reader to notice in this segment? and think as a result?

d) Why is the author telling the reader this information right now?

e) How does this information connect to what the author has already told the reader?

f) How is the text organized to reinforce key details and the main point the author is trying to make?

g) How does this information and the author's point connect to what the readers already know and issues they already care about?

h) Does the author tell the readers why we should think this way? Is the author direct or implicit about making her case?

i) Am I convinced or unconvinced by the author? Why?

j) How will this text inform how I think, read, act in the future?

Student QtA Talkback for *Don't Pat the Wombat* by Elizabeth Haney

Here's an example of fifth-grader Serena's talkback using the QtA prompts. The QtA was completed one-on-one with me after Serena read the book.

Start Off: Prompt a) Who is the author of this piece? And what do we know about this author?

> *The writer is Elizabeth Honey. It says inside the book cover that she is a popular children's author. From Australia. That's important since we are studying Australia. She mostly does picture books. And I see this book has photographs throughout of goofy people so maybe this is like a picture book for older kids. She has won awards. It says she likes humor so maybe this will be funny. I hope so.*

Prompt b) What might be her purpose and agenda in writing this text?

> *I think she wants us to have fun and maybe understand the goofy kids. I also think she is criticizing school, maybe showing how it could be different.*

Prompt c) What is the author writing about? i.e. what is the general topic or issue?

> *The topic of this book is about going to camp but there is this terrible chaperone called Mr. Crom The Bomb who wants to kill their fun so they are going to have to figure out how to deal with him. So maybe the topic is about dealing with adults who are a pain. I think the author wants us to have fun but also to see how to deal with problems.*

Prompt d) What important information does the author present? i.e. what are the key details?

> *I think the really key details are how Mr. Cromwell picks on the kids, particularly Jonah. And Jonah has a lot of secrets, bad things that happened to*

him that he is sad about. Mr. Cromwell always acts better than others and is mean. But when they [Jonah and Mr. C] canoe together Mr. Cromwell tries to scare Jonah and he falls out of the canoe and gets knocked unconscious. Jonah saves his life and has to walk back to camp. Mr. Cromwell leaves the camp and Jonah is a hero. Then he starts to tell some of his secrets to his friends, like that he had to put his dog to sleep. The rest of camp is fantastic. The whole canoe thing makes Mr. Cromwell change and he sends him this feather back that he just took from Jonah's hat which shows how he is being nicer and has changed. There are lots of other stories in the book but I think this is the most important.

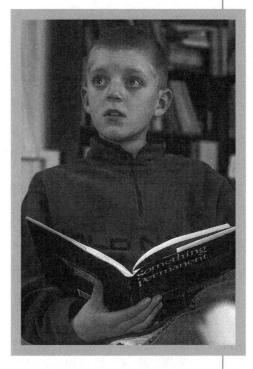

Nate questions author Cynthia Rylant about her views on the Depression and modern life as expressed in her book *Something Permanent*.

Prompt e) What is the author's point? i.e. what is the main idea or central focus? What conclusion do the key details add up to? What does the author want me to know, think, believe, or do?

I think the author is saying how one bad apple can ruin the whole bunch. One person can ruin a good time for everybody. But if you try to be good then maybe you can make it OK and get through to that person. It's hard to say, but I think that the author wants to tell me not to make fun of people and be hard on them because they are worth something and maybe have a secret life you don't know about... So I should be more understanding and try to make things better, not worse. And I think the author is saying that we all can do that, even if we think we can't.

Using the QtA prompts tunes students in to "the intelligence behind a text" who created the text and is trying to communicate something through it. It can also help students to explore areas of agreement or disagreement with authors on important topics.

GUIDELINES FOR DETERMINING AN AUTHOR'S MAIN IDEA

I developed the following set of guidelines with a group of seventh graders over several weeks. The process of creating such a list of problem-solving strategies is incredibly effective, so while you should use this example to guide your thinking, you should also invite students to collaborate on one of their own.

1. IDENTIFY THE TOPIC OF A PIECE

To find clues to topic:

a) Look at the title.

b) Look at the first and last paragraph—the topic is usually named.

c) Ask yourself: What is discussed throughout the whole selection? What subject spreads across the whole text?

d) Look at captions, pictures, words in bold, headings, and so forth for clues to topic. What do all of these have in common?

e) Remind yourself: The topic must include all the major details and events from the selection. *Caution:* Not every detail has something to do with the topic. The topic is the common element or connection between major details.

f) What do all major details share in common?

Check Yourself: It's Not the True Topic if...

a) It's too general or too big. (Topic statement suggests or could include many ideas not stated in the text.)

b) It's off the mark, totally missing the point.

c) It only captures one detail, rather than all of the key details.

d) It captures only some of the details, for example, maybe you didn't think about the ending.

Questions to Check Yourself:

a) Does the topic I've identified give an accurate picture of what the whole selection is about?

b) Was I as specific as possible?

c) After naming the topic, can I now specifically picture in my mind what happened or was communicated in the text? or might I picture something different that also fits my topic statement? If so, how can I change my topic statement to correct the problem?

2. IDENTIFY ALL DETAILS/MAJOR EVENTS
Authors often plant important ideas in:
   a) Details that reflect or refer to the title.
   b) Details at the beginning of a text.
   c) Details at the end.
   d) Surprises, revelations, whenever your expectations are not met.
   e) Repetition.
   f) Lots of attention given to a detail, for instance, long explanation or description.
   g) Subheads and italicized text.
   h) Changes in character, tone, mood, setting, plot twists.
   i) A question near the beginning or the end.

Check Yourself: It's Not a Key Detail if...
   a) It's interesting, but it doesn't develop the topic/lead to the central focus.
   b) It remind us of something and is even personally important, but if you were to remove it from the piece, the piece wouldn't lose any significant meaning or impact.

Questions to Check Yourself:
   a) Are all the details related to the topic?
   b) How do the key details relate to each other?
   c) What pattern do they make?
   d) What point do they repeat or add up to?

3. IDENTIFY THE CENTRAL FOCUS (the main idea or point the author makes about the topic):
   a) The statement of central focus you name must make a point about the topic and cover the whole selection.
   b) Ask yourself: Is the central focus directly stated? If not, it must be inferred.
   c) Which details help me decide on the central focus? Why are these details important?
   d) The central focus considers how the details relate to one another or lead to one another

(what caused or led to what).

e) The central focus must consider the ending and how the details or events led to this final conclusion.

Check Yourself: It's Not the Central Focus Statement if…

a) It is so literal and specific it doesn't allow the reader to apply the main idea to his own life.

b) It is too general—more like a topic statement than a main idea.

c) It is true but misses the point of the text. Wasn't what the author was talking about.

d) It misses the point.

e) It only fits one detail or event, not the whole text.

f) It does not incorporate all details.

g) It doesn't fit ending or final situation.

Questions to Check Yourself:

a) What point do the key details repeat and add up to?

b) Is the central focus a statement about the topic?

c) Is it something useful that can help you to think or act in the world?

d) Also consider: Do you agree with the statement as applied to life? Why or why not?

AUTHORIAL READING: CONTEMPLATING WHAT'S IN AN AUTHOR'S HEAD AND HEART

Researchers Rabinowitz and Smith urge us to aim high—to have our students become "authorial" readers. An authorial reader asks: What does this text mean to the audience it was written for, and how do I feel about that? Much like the kind of reading Beck et al. advocate in *Questioning the Author,* authorial reading is an active reading, a critical reading, a fiesty reading, if you will. Such a reader doesn't merely let a story wash over him, receiving a narrative much like a shore receives a wave, but *exercises* thought. He thinks about—and perhaps discusses with others—what a book's characters' seem to express about humanity, what the author meant to say about this larger world issue, and how he, the reader, feels about that. In short, these readers try to discern what the work implies about the state of humankind. What English teachers call "theme" can sometimes be pinned with one word, such as "justice"—which really refers to a topic; in contrast, an author's generalization implies propositions about the world and human beings. For example, a theme of *The Wombat* is relationships. The author's generalization proposes that adults who weild power disrespectfully over students will not be able to engage in fruitful relationships with them, and that the best relationships are those of mutual respect and support. The activities presented in the following sections help students converse with an author in various ways in order to become authorial readers and in so doing, attain a deeper level of comprehension.

Backtalks

Some teachers like to use a version of think-alouds called *talking back.* This technique is different from the think-alouds we've seen thus far, because students are stopped *after* reading a segment of text and asked to think back and report on what they noticed, thought, and did as they read. It's a reporting later instead of an as-it-happens account.

I created a variation I call *backtalk* in which students, after a segment of text that presents an argument, a piece of evidence, an interesting observation, or an opinion, converse with *the author* about their take on the information. They might choose to agree, disagree, keep an open mind, or add to the author's ideas. As students get better at this, I ask them to support their views on the issue with evidence from the text and beyond, as I'll explain in the next chapter.

When kids read stories, it works well to invite them to talk back to a character about something she has said, done, planned, or felt. Students enjoy providing alternative views or advice for the character and in the process deepen their understanding of the story. Or, as you saw in the drama example above, students can talk back to authors about how they have treated characters, and so on.

Talkbacks and backtalks tend to be shorter exercises than think-alouds. For example, if I'm reading aloud a novel, I might spontaneously ask kids to spend three to five minutes talking back about a particular passage in pairs or a small group. Talkbacks are guided, usually completed in response to a few prompts as in the case of the QtA. Backtalks are direct responses to a character's or author's actions and ideas. Backtalks work particularly well at the end of natural text segments, such as chapters or the end of books. Kids easily internalize the skills involved and become more adept and aware of monitoring their engagement, explaining it, and conversing with authors and ideas in "grand conversations" about ideas that affect them and the world they live in. This is an empowering and democratic move for student readers, particularly reluctant readers who may have spent many years disenfranchised by school and kept outside, as nonparticipants in the very conversations

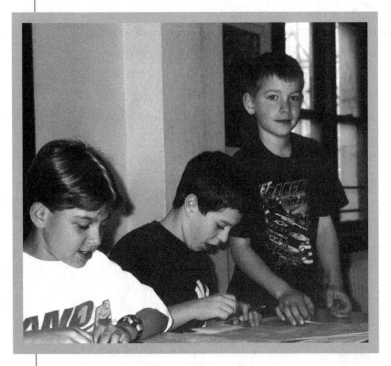

Fifth graders peruse the editorial page of a local newspaper, searching for a piece that captures their interest.

that do and will so profoundly affect them.

Op-ed pieces from the newspaper work particularly well for this. So do news articles or features about volatile subjects, particularly ones that quote people who come from different perspectives. Stories where characters have questionable views and take interesting or questionable actions are good too.

Sixth Graders Talk Back on *The Fighting Ground*

After reading the first few sections of Avi's *The Fighting Ground,* I asked my sixth graders to talk back to Jonathan. In this story, the main character Jonathan wants to fight in the Revolutionary War with the patriots and cannot believe that he and his father are staying home to tend the farm. When the bells ring to signal that the British are coming, Jonathan runs off to join the militia, and there his troubles begin.

To help my students out, I had one student play the part of Jonathan, and we physically put him in a *hot seat* in front of the classroom. (This is another drama strategy that helps students understand talking back to a character or author.) Most warned Jonathan not to go to the battle, some urging him to think of his father's wishes and others declaring that he should under no circumstances trust the colonel, giving many reasons for not doing so (which proved they were tuning in to characterization!). A few students told Jonathan he'd made a mistake but now he had to stick with it. These kids usually gave him some kind of advice about surviving the march and battle ahead (which showed they were paying attention to our lessons on prediction!).

In a journal entry following this activity, Jenny directed her comments at the author and scolded Avi. She was talking back to the author, telling him he had made a mistake sending a thirteen-year-old boy into battle. "That was mean," she wrote, "why not tell the story of his older brother? Jonathan is going to get squashed and it will be all your fault!" (Authors can also be put on the hot seat, and for variation, the characters and authors could even talk back to the readers who are questioning, judging, or advising them.)

On the following page you will find a checklist that students can use to both guide their backtalks and to assess how well they are recognizing craft and conversing with the authors about that craft and the ideas expressed through it.

Name _____ Date _____

Conversing with the Author Check Sheet

(✓+ for always, ✓ for sometimes, ✓- for not yet)

I, the reader:

____ notice/comment on the way a text is organized or the way in which information is withheld and presented

____ notice/comment on the words and vocabulary used

____ notice/comment on the style of the author

____ notice and identify conventions/textual codes used by the author

____ notice and comment on how conventions and constructions are used to make the author's point

____ evaluate the way the text is written

____ indicate some conception of the author, what kind of purpose she has in writing this text, what kind of person she might be, and so on

____ consider the author's meaning, the point being made through the text

____ indicate agreement, adaptation to, or argument with the author's meaning

____ indicate reason for agreement or disagreement

____ indicate ways in which story meaning may inform my own thinking and action

Which of these moves did you make in your latest backtalk? Give examples. Which ones did you not try but think you might like to try with your next reading?

Improving Comprehension with Think-Aloud Strategies • Scholastic Professional Books

CHAPTER 6

NEW GENRES, NEW READING MOVES:
Using Think-Alouds to Teach Students About Text Types and Text Features

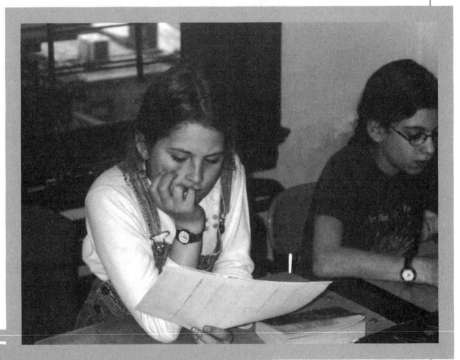

A student reads a ballad. When students arrive in the intermediate grades, the kinds of texts we ask them to read are often new to them and require them to employ specialized stragies that they probably do not yet know.

Recently, our family was watching the movie *Chariots of Fire*, which won an Oscar for Best Picture in the early '80s. My daughters became mightily confused within the first few scenes and we had to continually pause the videotape to explain things.

I soon realized that they had two problems that were keeping them from getting the film. The first was that they did not have the background to understand the situation of the story. Readers simply cannot comprehend what they do not already know something about. If you don't know anything at all about a topic, you have no traction—no possibility of comprehending. (This is the basic insight of cognitive psychology's schema theory.)

So my wife and I explained to our girls a bit about World War I and how the Versailles Treaty led in many ways to World War II. We reminded the girls that many of their relatives had fought in both wars, and some had been stationed in England, where the movie takes place. We talked about the period between the wars as a time of a crisis of faith, the rise of nationalism, the persecution of people who were perceived as different. "This movie," my wife told the girls, "is really about how two athletes, one Christian and one Jewish, expressed who they were and overcame the personal challenges of their era through sport." The girls asked a few more questions and nodded that they understood.

A second and equally profound challenge was that the girls had not recognized the organizational form of the movie and how the film's structure asked them to frame their own response and interpretation. The girls did not understand who the characters were or why the film continually switched from one group of people to another.

Authors of texts typically "tip-off" a reader or viewer about structure early on. An author of an argument or opinion piece, for instance, explicitly or implicitly states at the outset a thesis or claim—a position that he/she will attempt to prove in the course of the piece. This claim is a tip-off of the text's purpose, how it will be organized, and how it should be read. Readers need to learn to notice the tip-off and to mobilize the reading operations that such a text will require. Authors of stories tip off their readers about their structure in various ways, most simply with "Once upon a time" or a more sophisticated variant. For example, they might present some characters faced with a problematic situation. Readers are thus tipped off that the narrative will lead toward resolution. The point of view is another tip-off, letting us know whose perspectives and story we will be hearing. When points of view are alternated, the reader knows she is to compare and contrast the perspectives and stories. This is the case with *Chariots of Fire*, in which the whole structure, plot, and point of the movie are driven by the viewer successfully comparing the similarities and differences in the two characters' experiences.

The "tip-off" was that we were introduced to one character, Harold Abraham, as he arrives at Cambridge University. Then we immediately switch to Eric Liddell's arrival home in Scotland. Then we are back to Abraham's orientation to Caius College, switching immediately to Liddell's welcome home. Then to Abraham's first competition at Cambridge, the race against the clocktower. And back to Liddell's first running race in Scotland. I told the girls that whenever a text switches from one thing to another and then back again, this is a tip-off that the author or producer ("the intelligence behind the text") is inviting us to compare and contrast the two people, issues, or situations being juxtaposed. The girls understood and later in the movie were able to identify the topic and salient features of each scene, thereby understanding the implicit comparison *and* the point made by each comparison. This allowed them to see how different aspects of each athlete's experience were being contrasted: their motivation, their training styles, how they dealt with the women in their lives, their friends and support group, the role of faith, and much more.

The girls then considered what they could learn from these contrasts. At the end, Fiona said, "I like them both. I thought they were both great runners and good people. They were just different. And so they had to deal with their problems different too." Jasmine disagreed, "I thought Eric [Liddell] was happier and loved running more. At the end he celebrates and the other guy [Abraham] doesn't. I think we were supposed to like them both, but admire him [Liddell] more. He ran for joy, not to win, so he was happier."

Tipping the girls off to the movie's structure allowed them to understand how the movie was constructed, helped them to see points of comparison and contrast, and helped them to name and talk about various issues raised by the movie (like the role of faith in one's life, or the rise of scientific sports training and professional coaching). Understanding the content, the form, and how the form invited them to respond and interpret the story helped them to talk about, consider, and deeply understand the movie's themes.

Understanding Text and Task Expectations

A plethora of research indicates that student interest in reading, amount of time spent in reading activity, and reading achievement fall off after fourth or fifth grade (see, e.g.,

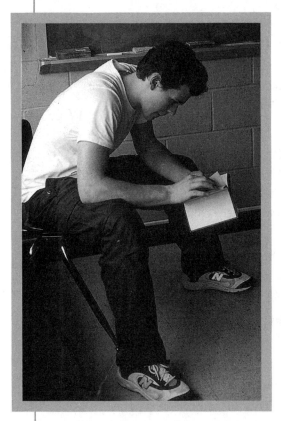

To play the reading game, you gotta know the rules laid down by the text you are reading.

Heathington, 1979; McKenna, Ellsworth, and Kear, 1995; Shapiro and White, 1991). My own research has convinced me that part of the reason is that we stop teaching how to read at precisely the time that students move from an almost singular emphasis on reading narrative texts (both fictional and informational) to much more of an emphasis on reading kinds of texts with structures, conventions, and expectations with which they are unfamiliar (Wilhelm, Baker, Dube, 2001).

Specifically, as students continue through school, the narratives they read become more sophisticated. Straightforward stories become less straightforward, with unreliable narrators, implied main ideas and themes, the use of symbolism, flashbacks, and inference gaps. Similarly, rhyming poems and lyric poems may give way to ironic monologues, free verse, ballads, sonnets, villanelles, and so forth.

Informational text in a variety of structures also becomes more important. Students are expected to read to learn information, presented in a variety of formats, which they are expected to understand well enough that they can apply or use it, hopefully even evaluate and critique it.

Just as my daughters were confused by *Chariots of Fire,* our students become disoriented when they are thrown into reading a new kind of text without assistance. As teachers, we have to provide them with on-point instruction so that they can get their bearings. In this chapter, we will look at the specific demands of some common text types and how talk-backs or cued think-alouds can help students to recognize and meet those demands.

First, what is a "text type"? I consider a "text type" to be synonymous with "genre." I agree with literary theorists like Jonathan Culler (1975) and Peter Rabinowitz (1987) who define a genre (or text-type) as any set of texts that share the same expectations of readers. In other words, if a reader has to notice the same codes, meet the same demands, and read two texts in the same ways using the same interpretive operations, then these two texts belong to the same genre or class of text-types. These theorists argue that one of the problems posed for teachers and students is that we typically construe genres too broadly. For instance, many anthologies define "poetry" as a genre. But lyric poetry, for example, uses totally different codes and structures than other kinds of poetry. To help readers, we need to slice genres more finely, into text-types like lyric poetry, ironic monologues, and concrete poems—groups of texts that share characteristics and expectations.

Planning Your Genre Instruction: Tools That Help

So how do you figure out what expectations particular kinds of text-types make on readers? One way to do it is to do think-alouds of your own or to study those of your students so that you can see what the successful readers do and the less successful ones miss when reading a particular type of text.

Another way is to use the "inquiry square" which I have adapted from the work of George Hillocks. Basically, this square (see sample, next page) is a problem-solving guide that can help you think through what is required to write—and therefore read—a particular kind of text. It guides teachers to think through the four kinds of knowledge readers (and writers) must use when comprehending text:

1. Procedural knowledge of substance (knowing the process of activating or finding the background information you need).

2. Procedural knowledge of form (knowing the process of using structural conventions).

3. Declarative knowledge of form (being able to declare the text type and how it works).

4. Declarative knowledge of substance (being able to declare the meaning of the text and how the structure helped to communicate it).

Understanding Unreliable Narrators (Smith, 1991, NCTE) offers a clear discussion of the specific expectations that ironic narratives place on readers and a practical sequence of texts and activities that can teach students how to read irony and judge unreliable narrators. This text also offers an excellent example of sequencing instruction so that students learn text-by-text and activity-by-activity, with responsibility and expertise gradually handed over to the students. See also Smith, 1989, on teaching students how to read irony in poetry. George Hillocks (1995) takes a close look at the demands of fable writing, satires, and argument writing in his book *Teaching Writing as Reflective Practice* (NCTE).

Inquiry Square

Reproduce this square to help you plan your teaching of a genre that is unfamiliar to your students. Remember that like any reader, students must use all four kinds of knowledge as they read!

1. What is the purpose for reading or writing this kind of text?

	Procedural Knowledge	Declarative Knowledge
S U B S T A N C E	2. How can students be helped to get the stuff? i.e., access the necessary background information and knowledge that must be brought to bear?	4. How can students be helped to articulate the meaning of the text?
F O R M	3. How can students be helped to put the content they are reading into a mental structure suggested by the author?	5. How can students be helped to name the structure of the text and how this construction helped communicate the author's meaning?

Or, you might instead brainstorm genre elements lists like those that follow. The lists will get you started in thinking about the expectations of certain text types and in turn, how you might highlight them for students.

Task-Specific or Text-Specific? Teasing Apart Two Terms

I've already blown a lot of hot air earlier in this book about task-specific expectations, but let me review here. A task-specific expectation is when an author uses a particular kind of convention, like irony or symbolism, or when a text is written in such a way that requires a reader to make inferences or find an implied central focus. These conventions, and their associated "task" for the reader trying to interpret and make meaning of them, can move across text types. For example, symbolism is often used in lyric poetry, short stories and novels, and sometimes even in informational writing. Inferring is a task required by most literature and is required much less in informational texts, where everything important is to be made clear.

When a text-type generally uses a particular kind of convention (leading to a task-specific expectation of the reader) then that task is considered to be one of the text-type or genre expectations. So task-specific processes are subsets of text-specific processes. Task-specific processes may move across text types as in the case of symbolism. Most text-types require the same task-specific processes every time you read that genre, and quite often these processes are unique to reading this kind of text, as you will see below when we explore reading fables and arguments, as well as other texts. A text structure (like cause and effect or comparison-contrast) is a structural convention that is often associated with a particular text type but could also move across and be embedded in other text types. For example, narrative most often uses the text structure of chronological order, but chronological order is also used in how-to descriptions and other kinds of texts. Classification can be considered a kind of genre when the whole text is structured by divisions or "classes" of information, but it can also be an embedded structure in another genre, such as an argument.

The Inquiry Square: A Teacher's Example

	Declarative Knowledge	Procedural Knowledge
F O R M	Student names the features of the fable including animals as symbols of foibles, ends in moral, etc.	How to put the substance of the proposed fable in an appropriate form: What animals could represent the foible and other contrasting values? What actions and key details could show the consequences of this foible? Events must be a syllogism leading to a conclusion that can be summarized as a moral.
S U B S T A N C E	Knowledge of the content of particular fables.	How to produce the substance of fables: brainstorming for human qualities that are immoral or irritating. Generate foibles and their concomitant actions, etc. Choose a big one that causes problems for self and others. Choose a foible that is correctable Think about how people with this foible act.

- Why write or read this kind of text?
- How can we get the "stuff" to write or read this? (Inquiry?)
- What do we have to do with the "stuff" to make it an argument, satire, table, etc.?

GENRE CHARACTERISTICS CHART

Following is an overview of some genres (text-types) that are often read by students and the task-specific processes a reader uses to read them. As you introduce a genre to kids, develop such lists of characteristics with your students. Through think-alouds and other lessons, model how you pay attention to these features to help you read and enjoy the text.

Mystery

The Basic Definition

- A subgenre of narrative fiction; often thought of as a detective story.
- Usually involves a mysterious death or a crime to be solved. In a closed circle of suspects, each suspect must have a credible motive and a reasonable opportunity for committing the crime. The central character must be a detective who eventually solves the mystery by logical deduction from facts fairly presented to the reader. This classic structure is the basis for hundreds of variations on the form.

Purpose

To engage in and enjoy solving a puzzle. Explore moral satisfaction (or dissatisfaction) at resolution. Consider human condition and how to solve or avoid human problems.

Tip-Offs (also known as rules of notice)

- Mystery, crime, or another puzzle to be solved.

- Main character who is a detective who sets out to solve a mystery.
- Suspects and their motives; these must be weighed and evaluated.
- Overt Clues about the crime are presented.
- Hidden Evidence is presented, i.e., essential details are offered in such a way that they seem unimportant.
- Inference Gaps—mysteries, by their very nature, do not tell the whole story. It is up to readers to notice the gaps in the story and try to fill these gaps by using and connecting the information that is presented.
- Suspense—having to hold various possible conclusions at bay as you wait to see what happens; reader is expected to enjoy the suspense, and to read to find out what will happen.
- Foreshadowing—clues left by the author as to possible outcomes.
- Red herring—a kind of foreshadowing clue that leads the reader to false conclusions.

What a Mystery Requires of a Reader

The reader's job is to put the puzzle pieces offered by the author together to figure out the mystery, to appreciate the detective's craft, and to take moral satisfaction from the solution to the mystery. To do this, readers must notice and make meaning with the codes offered above, i.e., they must notice the various forms of evidence and evaluate them; they must notice inference gaps and try to fill them.

Biography

The Basic Definition

- A subgenre of narrative nonfiction/historical nonfiction.

- Presents the facts about an individual's life and makes an attempt to interpret those facts, explaining the person's feelings and motivations. Good biographers use many research tools to gather and synthesize information about their subject, including the person's words, actions, journals, reactions, related books, interviews with friends, relatives, associates and enemies, historical context, psychology, primary source documents.

Purpose

Often to understand the person and the events and history affected by that person.

Tip-Offs

- Often starts with birth or early life and often covers birth-to-death.

- Often delves in to a person's formative years, exploring early influences on a subject's later life.

- Situates person's life in historical terms and a cultural context.

- Uses direct quotes from person and those who knew her.

- Sometimes uses fictionalized scenes/dialogues but always based on what is known about the person and the events described.

- Often uses pictures, maps, photographs, or other historically available documents.

- Biographer possesses a point of view, a larger agenda, and a purpose in reporting on the person's life.

What a Biography Requires of a Reader

Reader should consider author's purpose in presenting the biography. Is it idealized? fair? Why or why not? Is bio a hatchet job? Why? Who is the biographer? When was this biography written? How does this affect my reading of it? How does this help me to understand the influence of this person on history, and history and culture's effect on her? How might this person be a model for things to do or not do in my own life?

Tall Tales

The Basic Definition

A subgenre of narrative fiction/folktales. One of four categories of folktales generally recognized by folklorists. (Others are the variants of European folktales, such as Jack and the Beanstalk, the folktales of African Americans that grew out of African and European roots; and the tales of Native American groups) Tall tales include "exuberant combinations of fact with outrageous fiction." The tales feature an "improvement" on actual happenings. The contrast between fact and fiction is enhanced by giving the story a realistic framework and by a deadpan storytelling style.

Purpose

To entertain, celebrate cleverness of hero, imagine "What If?" and show resilience of group he represents.

Tip-Offs

- Realism combined with outrageous exaggeration.
- Often reflects the hardships endured by the American settlers.
- Heroes embody courage, brute force, cleverness, as well as the virtues of thrift, hard work, and perseverance.

Fables

The Basic Definition

A short tale used to teach a moral lesson, often with animals as characters.

Purpose

To instruct, to teach humans a lesson about recognizing and overcoming their foibles; to critique authority figures in humorous and anonymous ways; to poke fun.

Tip-Offs

- The story is very brief.
- Main characters are usually animals and are characterized quickly with a few broad strokes.
- One animal/character usually displays the vice or foible being critiqued. This foible is what brings embarassment or a downfall to the character and this conclusion leads directly to the moral, which follows the fable and is stated in one sentence.

What a Fable Requires of a Reader

The reader must pay attention to the title, which will cue who or what to pay attention to. Then the reader must figure out the symbolic value of each animal or character—what human trait does each represent? The reader must recognize introductory situation and what causes the complication and consequences. He reads moral and understands how the events of the story, particularly the conclusion, lead to and mirror the instructive statement summarized by the moral. Reader should consider how the moral might apply to her own life.

Arguments

The Basic Definition

The process of presenting or comprehending a reasoned case.

Purpose

To inquire into problems and possible solutions, to persuade or convince others to change belief or take action, to try and get one's way!

Tip-Offs

- A need or desire for something new or for something to change is expressed.
- This assertion is supported through the use of evidence and warrants explaining how the evidence leads to this claim.
- Something is being promoted. (Advertisements almost always contain an argument. Argument is incorporated into many forms of propaganda and persuasion.)

What an Argument Requires of a Reader

The reader must first understand what is being claimed and what is at stake. What will happen or follow if we agree with or reject the argument? If others agree with or reject the argument? Then the reader must recognize and evaluate the evidence and

how it is explained or linked to the claim. The reader may want to express reservations and see if these are or could be responded to. Ultimately, the reader must decide if she is compelled by the argument and if so, what she should believe and do as a result.

Satires

The Basic Definition

A text that uses irony, sarcasm, and ridicule to expose and make fun of human folly and vice.

Purpose

To critique the status quo, to make fun of others and the self, and to offer renewed alternatives and possibilities for being different.

Tip-Offs

- Something is being made fun of, irony is being used, there is a tone of mockery or derision, perhaps the author seems to be supporting a point of view that you cannot expect her to seriously support.

What a Satire Requires of a Reader

The reader must discern what is being made fun of and what possible alternatives are being offered. The reader must decide what is not under dispute in the text, what is under dispute, and how to reconstruct the real implied meaning behind the false satiric meanings being literally presented by the author.

HELPING KIDS READ GENRES THAT ARE NEW TO THEM: THE BASICS

Whether you use an inquiry square, a genre chart, or something else altogether to plan your teaching, the important step is to read through several examples of a text-type

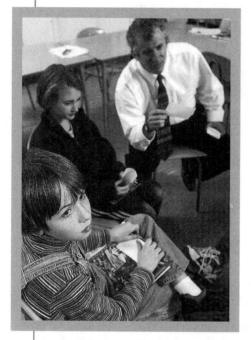

Here we collaboratively create an argument using notecards that feature different elements of an argument.

carefully before giving an example of it to students, thinking through all the knowledge and processes you are using to comprehend it. Then, you will probably plan your teaching along these lines:

- Read several examples with the entire class.
- Do a think-aloud or a talkback of some kind.
- Figure out what is always required of readers of that genre.

When you introduce a new text type, simplify it to its most basic structures and features. These are what you will first teach students to attend to. Later, more sophisticated features—and the ways to interpret and critique them—can be introduced.

- Practice using the moves that are required by the genre.
- Try to write an example of the text type using all the conventions required by that genre. Model this for students (you might collaborate on one as a class) before inviting them to do it.

Reading Fables: An Example of Teaching a Genre

A fable is a good genre to teach because it is accessible and because fables are usually short, so students can gain lots of practice with various examples in a brief amount of time. Through lots of practice with short works you can build students' skills for use in longer works. For example, the text demands of fables include task-specific processes such as interpreting symbolism and reading for a main idea that can transfer to many other kinds of reading. If kids have trouble or make mistakes, it's not a big deal; you can help correct the problems and quickly move on to another example.

Fables address concepts about central human issues and concerns, of course, and thus easily fit into units of study. Fables are also fabulous (if you'll excuse the etymological pun!) for teaching main idea or central focus because they lead pointedly to a moral, which is usually expressed. Morals can be deleted and students can write their own and debate relative merits of how well each one summarizes the implications and central focus of the fable. Fables also show students how stories can be used to make points and cases for particular ways of thinking and being—which we might embrace or disagree with—and therefore encourage authorial reading.

So, the first thing I do with my students is to ask: What is it that you have to know and do to write or read a fable? With this question in mind, I have them read two or three fables and then spend a few minutes brainstorming in their notebooks possible purposes of writing a fable. Here's the conversation my students and I had after they read "The Man With Two Wives," "Venus and the Cat," and "The Lion in Love" and brainstormed about both the purposes of the fables and the features that they all shared.

Tony: Well, fables are good for making fun of mistakes.

Melissa: And more than that… the mistakes they repeat. Their screw-ups, their personality defects.

Tom: I think the point is to understand our faults so we can make them better.

JW: Excellent! So fables might help us improve, or tell others how to improve! [Jeff writes all ideas on board.]

Joe: They all end with a bang.

Melissa: And that ending leads to the point—the part that tells you what you should do.

JW: The moral.

Melissa: Yeah….

JW: [A bit later in conversation] Okay, now we have a good list of some of the possible purposes of writing and reading fables, and we've decided we're going to write some fables to draw attention to problems in the school. Before we get started, what do we have to think about?

Jayne: Who's gonna read these?

JW: Right. Who will be the audience?

Jamal: And why will they read them and what do we want to happen because they read them?

Riley: Hey, jump back! What are the issues we're going to write about? We never talked about that!

Jamal: And what we want to change! If it's something that can't be changed, then why write the fable?

Riley: You da man, Jamal! But how we gonna know if the thing can be changed or not?

JW: By doing a little bit of research!

Students: [Groan!]

Jamal: You mean talk to the principal and stuff?

The students did an excellent job of figuring out purposes of fables and then began to figure out how to decide what to write about and how to get the information they needed (the procedural knowledge of substance).

As we then brainstormed how to put what they might learn into the form of a fable, they brainstormed these ideas, which I wrote on the board:

Figure out animals or other characters that suggest various human values, including the foibles to be addressed. (symbolism)

Animals must exhibit human values but not be humans (not smoke cigars or drink coffee).

Figure out a sequence of events involving the characters that will make a particular point about the consequences of certain attitudes or behaviors.

Title that describes the main character and his or her problem or that describes the problem or issue being examined.

Begin fable by introducing situation.

Immediately proceed to complication, the problem or issue at play.

Major character makes decision or takes action.

Decision or action leads to a clear set of consequences.

The action of the story and its consequences imply a clear moral.

This syllogism of events leading to a conclusion must be summarized in a moral.

What makes a good moral? We must consider phrasing and content.

To conclude the day's lesson, I asked students to think about what we would expect our readers to do as they read our fables and how we were going to help them do these things.

Talkbacks

Sometimes I have students do a think-aloud of the text-type I'm introducing. Because fables are short, students might read several and compare to find what moves and strategies are always required. Or different students could read different fables and strategies could be compared.

Another option is to have students read one and then do a talkback of their reading. Here's a general guide for such a talkback, along with some of Jamal's specific comments during a talkback about Aesop's "The Man with Two Wives." I always organize talkbacks along the four dimensions of activity highlighted by the inquiry square (see page 140). Jamal's responses to the prompts he was given are in italics:

TALKBACK FOR FABLE READING
(The talkback enacts procedural knowledge of substance.)

1. The talkback reflects knowledge of the topic.
e.g., What was the topic of the fable, the problem or issue it examines?
This fable is about a dude who had two wives. He took too much on his plate. It's kind of like about what Jesus said about serving two masters!!! You just canna do it!

2. The talkback connects the student's prior knowledge to the text.
e.g., What background knowledge about the topic helped me to read this? What did I have to know and bring to the text so it would make sense and connect to my life and activity?
When I read this I thought about when I tried to run track and play baseball at the same time last spring… Different kinds of friends and they want to do different things.
(Jamal uses procedural knowledge of substance by accessing his relevant experiences.)

3. The talkback recognizes and names global (and perhaps local, embedded) structures and conventions of the text.
e.g., I knew it was a fable because…

Because it was a fable it started by…

> *I knew this was a fable because we been studying them. Plus it started with a title, was really short, it didn't have any animals which is kind of funny, but it had this guy who made a big mistake and his two wives kept takin' bites out of him and it had a little old moral at the end and that clinches it. It's a fable. We're supposed to learn from his mistakes being held up to the old microscope.*

(Jamal taps into declarative knowledge of form by recognizing and articulating the genre tip-offs and expectations. He begins to consider procedural knowledge of form—what you do to respond to particular structures and codes.)

4. The talkback includes references to the process of reading.

e.g., When I read this, I was sure to do certain things as a reader like ___.

Because it was a fable and I know the animals are symbolic of human foibles, I figured out that the fox symbolized being sly or cunning ___.

A part that was hard for me to understand was… so I ___.

I reread the part about… because ___.

> *I was lookin' for the lesson from the very start. I knew somebody was gonna make a big mistake and get squeezed and go down and that Aesop was gonna pass big-time judgement on him!*

(Jamal uses procedural knowledge of form because he recognizes the form and initiates processes for fulfilling the formal expectations, i.e., appreciating how the events lead to the moral.)

5. The talkback includes an adequate retelling of surface and deep meaning.

It summarizes the key points to remember, including:

    — introduction to situation

    — key details; main events and consequences of them

    — a moral and how it follows from the story action

    — is in your own words, though vocabulary from the story may be used.

> *This guy married two babes, one old and one young. I don't know how he swung that, but he did. But the problems started because the young one pulled out his grey hairs cause she didn't want him lookin like some old dude. But the old one pulled out his black hairs because she didn't want him lookin' young and sexy like me, I'm guessing!*

So the guy ends up bald. So the moral follows on all of that… you try to do too much,
you get pulled too many ways, then you lose whatever you had.

(Jamal uses declarative knowledge of substance by articulating the surface and deep meaning of the fable, which he was able to deduce by using the required reading processes.)

Reading News Stories

News writing is a kind of simple informational writing that students need to know how to read for real-life purposes. I think that it is very important that students from upper elementary on become familiar with the newspaper and its various kinds of stories. The most basic story, of course, is the news story. I use news stories throughout my teaching to connect our studies to current events, to add new information and breadth to our classroom inquiries, and to teach reading strategies. I also often have students write news stories about their reading, since it gives such great practice in identifying key details, writing summaries, considering deep meaning, etc.

The conventions of news writing range from the simple to the more complex.

On the declarative level, student writers need to know that news is a report about a recent and noteworthy event, that it must include the five W's and H (who, what, where, why, when, and how) to comprehensively cover the event, that the purpose is to interest and inform the reader, that there are structural elements such as the headline, the lead, the body, and possible other elements such as quotations, call-outs, and so on.

On the procedural level, writers need to know how to inquire into the events and issues they will report on… through investigation, interviewing, databases, fact files, and more. They need to know what constitutes unbiased, comprehensive reporting and what does not. They need to learn how to put the substance they have learned into a form including a headline, lead, a body that covers the five W's and H, and so forth.

Later on, they'll learn about different kinds of news stories, like special kinds of news such as the death story, the meeting story, the sports story, the advance or follow-up story, and variations and extensions on the news like features, editorials, and reviews, all of which have particular purposes and codes.

Once they understand how such stories are produced, they will know what to attend to and critique as readers. At first, though, I attend to the general news story.

Questions to Guide Reading General News Stories

1. What's the topic of the article?

   The main topic of this article is ____. Tip-offs: The headline and first paragraph confirm this topic by ____.

2. What important ideas are expressed about the topic?

   The five W's and H are ____. The most important ideas to remember are ____.

3. Does it clearly make known how this event/issue relates to other events and issues, in the past and future? In other words, does it have important "global" implications? How should it help me think about things that are important?

   This article was important to read because ____. It connects to and will influence future issues like ____ by ____.

4. Is the story coherent? Do all the story ideas relate to each other?

   The ideas covered were all about making the point that ____. This helps the reader to understand that ____ were organized around the central issue of ____.

5. What reading strategies am I using to create meaning? What tools am I using as I critique the structure, the writing, or the content of the piece?

   When I read this article I had to do certain things as a reader, such as ____.

News stories are a type of general expository text that lays out information. Because news stories are short, students can get repeated practice with techniques that can help them in reading more extended informational texts, such as textbooks. The following guide can be used to help students with any kind of expository text.

Questions to Guide Reading General Exposition/Information Texts

1. What's the topic?

   This text was about the topic of ____.

2. What's the author's purpose?

   The author probably wrote this for the purpose of ____.

3. How does the structure of the piece serve its purpose? How does the organization of the piece serve the purpose?

   The author chose the form of ____ to meet her purpose because ____.

4. What are its main points?

The main points the author wants us to remember and carry away with us are ___.

5. What new ideas does it convey? What parts interested me?
   Ideas that I learned that surprised and interested me were ___.

6. What did I do as I read to help me understand? What did I do as I critiqued it?
   Things I did that helped me read this text and figure out what I thought about it were ___.

7. After reading the text, what questions do I want to ask the author?
   I'd like to ask the author some additional questions, and I'd like to know more about ___ and know what she thinks about ___ and ask why she wrote it in this particular way ___.

8. What does this piece do for me? How does it change my thinking about this topic or other topics? How does it influence my own future?
   I'm going to use this text to think about/write about/do these things ___.

Obviously, not all prompts need to be used or responded to, and prompts can be rephrased and adapted depending on the text or level of your students.

LOOKING AT THE ELEMENTS OF ARGUMENT

Perhaps the most important kind of text to be able to read or write is the argument. Newspapers, textbooks, magazines, and Web sites are full of arguments. Advertisements are perhaps the most ubiquitous form of argument. Think-alouds can be used to figure out what must be done to recognize, read, and critique an argument.

Now, arguments can seem daunting to teach and read, but I have found that the fourth and fifth graders with whom I work are able to understand and use arguments with great facility. So hang on and bear with me here!

According to the logician Stephen Toulmin and other philosophers of argument, on the basic level, arguments consist of a claim, data, and warrants. (I'm grateful to George Hillocks, 1995; Michael Smith, 1998; and to Maine Writing Project Fellow Lori Power, who adapted George's and Michael's ideas in the following way to create a teaching demonstration on reading advertisements as argument. The five questions in bold on page 158 are from Michael Smith's presentation. The animal rights examples are from Lori's presentation.)

To simplify the terms a bit: an argument starts with a claim, a position that will be argued for. This is also known as a thesis. With younger students, instead of using the

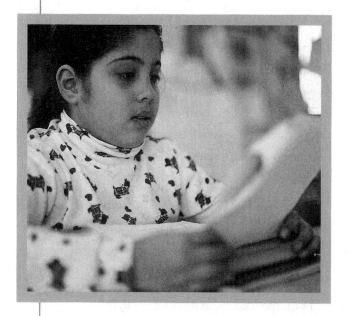

term "claim" I might just ask: What is your point? What are you arguing for?

Data is simply evidence. Any facts that can be used to support (or not support) the claim can be considered data. The younger students I work with all understand the word *evidence,* though I tend to use the term *data* with older students. Warrants are explanations of how the evidence supports the claim. With younger students I simply ask them to "explain the evidence."

Arguments begin and are grounded in evidence. The situation (data) provides the reason to make an argument in the first place. That is, there is a problem and we need to do something. The evidence (data) supports the claim about what needs to be done. Arguments are generally made because conditions cause us to desire something we lack or threaten something we value. Since data specify these conditions, they are the concrete facts and details indicating that things aren't as they should be or that they could be different.

For example, in an elementary school where I sometimes work, the students wanted a different lunch menu. Their evidence of the need for a different menu was a survey they took showing that many students did not eat hot lunch, or ended up not eating lunch at all, because the food was unappetizing, designated as "gross" or "yucky" in their survey. The administration cited evidence that the menu the students wanted (pizza from Pizza Hut, a salad bar) would cause the price of lunch to go up and that this would exclude still more students from affording hot lunch.

In another example important to my middle school students—the issue of animal rights in medical research—researchers think there is a problem, namely that new laws are keeping them from doing their research and fulfilling the purpose of their research. To argue against controls on their research they might cite the fact that particular regulations exist that keep them from using animals for their research (this is evidence). Opponents might cite figures on the death rate, suffering, and living conditions of laboratory animals and argue that the evidence shows the regulations are necessary to protect the animals. The regulations and statistics are evidence. When we come across evidence in an argument, it should prompt us to ask the author, "What makes you say so? What about your evidence supports your position?"

A claim is the thesis or point of the argument, also known as an assertion or proposition that the argument intends to establish. It implies action. In the school lunch argument, the students wanted a new lunch menu. In the animal rights argument, researchers claim that restrictions should be lifted. Animal rights advocates might claim that restrictions should be retained or strengthened.

Warrants are essential to arguments because they link the data (evidence) to the claim, and show how data leads to the claim. They explain how the evidence fits the claim and a prevailing set of higher beliefs, principles, and values. Many arguments are "unwarranted," which means that the data are not clearly linked to the claim. Such arguments are weak.

Strong arguments are based on beliefs, values, and principles with which the audience can agree. These shared convictions and the explanation of how they support the data and link it to the claim are the argument's warrants or evidence explanations. For example, in the debate on school lunch, the students might depend on the warrants that 1) students should eat lunch so they can be alert in the afternoon and remain healthy and 2) that students will tend to eat what is appetizing to them and refuse to eat what is not. Given the evidence from their survey, the students might argue that we must get more kids to eat lunch and that the menu must be changed to achieve this end.

In the debate on animals, researchers might depend on two warrants: 1) animal suffering is not as great an evil as human suffering, and 2) cures for diseases must be found as quickly as possible. Given the data showing extensive restrictions on animal research, these beliefs lead to the claim that the restrictions, which increase the cost and slow research, are bad policies that should be lifted. On the other hand, advocates for animal rights might depend on entirely different warrants: 1) humans are morally responsible for all their fellow creatures, or even 2) animals should have the same rights as humans. Readers should examine the author's evidence explanation (warrants) and ask if they explain "So What?" about the data.

Students are often surprised to learn that the same data can support entirely different claims, depending on the warrants—the explanations invoked and cultural values linked to the data.

Model the Process

Modeling how you attend to these features of argument in your own think-alouds helps students understand what to notice and how to judge and interpret these conventions. Cueing students to attend to claims, data, and warrants in their own think-alouds and helping them to ask the right questions about these features help them to become critical consumers of arguments.

For Students Well-Versed in the Elements of Argument

A bit more advanced argument may include backing, reservations, or qualifiers; and a response to reservations or rebuttal. But again, I would not pursue these more sophisticated conventions with students until they have mastered the basic ones. If some students are ready for these more advanced features, then I would certainly introduce these to them as I continued to work with other students on the basic features.

Backing is used when a warrant needs support. Readers ask an author: "How do you know the backing supports the truth of the warrant?"

Backing is used if the warrant is not familiar or compelling to the audience. For instance, animal rights activists must confront a very powerful argument by medical researchers that testing on animals is warranted by the value of human life. They may need to back their own warrants by convincing the audience that when we cherish the lives of all creatures, great and small, we deepen and enrich our own lives and increase the value of human life. Medical researchers, on the other hand, might back their warrant by citing evidence of human suffering that was alleviated, diseases cured, lives extended as a result of their research, and evidence that human suffering continues in many cases because of animal rights. There is a current television ad campaign in which drug companies use just such backing.

Reservations are arguments against the claim. The arguer may want to address these up front with a response. Readers must ask: "Are all reservations addressed?" and: "Does the response adequately address the reservation?"

Qualifiers are limits placed on the argument; for instance, if there are limits to the claim or if it applies only in certain instances. For example, researchers might qualify their argument to ensure the humane care of animals as long as it does not impede research. Animal rights advocates may grant the qualification that when humanity is in dire need, researchers might temporarily suspend certain restrictions.

INTRODUCING ARGUMENT:
SIXTH GRADERS TALK BACK TO MADISON AVENUE

The sixth grade is involved in a unit about the environment, and we're studying argument because we are all going to write arguments about an ecological topic of interest to us.

To study argument, we've been looking at advertisements to tease out the argument that each one makes. Here's Carrie having a go at an ad she found in *People* persuading readers to subscribe to *Money* magazine. She's using a talkback guide to help her identify the tip-off that the ad's structure is an argument and to help her identify and evaluate elements of an argument like claims, data, and warrants. The guide helps readers to recognize and interpret important genre conventions, thereby guiding their reading and critique of a particular text.

IDEA BOX

Have kids practice reading different text types and structures through the simplest and shortest possible texts. They might name the argument in an advertisement or editorial, discern the satire or irony in cartoons, or explore the comparison/contrast structure of before-and-after photographs in magazines.

All it says is, 'Why live paycheck to paycheck when you can live dividend to dividend?' And then it says, 'Money. You need this magazine.' Okay, that's the tip-off. They want us to buy the magazine. I think the claim is that we . . . lack money. Ha! They're right about that! No... the claim is ...errr. That we need Money... *the magazine, I mean. Because if you read* Money *then, ummm, you will earn so much from investing that you'll be all set. Yeah. Okay, as for data... what makes me think this claim is right? What supports it? Well, there... geezum... there isn't any data. There isn't anything! There's no warrants either... there's nothing that explains the data... But then there isn't any data, just a claim!!! This ad is just a claim. There's nothing that supports it. There is no reason in the world I should believe this ad. I wonder why they think this kind of ad would even work?*

Carrie exhibits here a knowledge of how arguments work and can see that this ad makes an implicit argument through a simple suggestion that it does not back up.

Here's an example of an argument from a student editorial (Michael Smith, 1998):

Claim: (Reader recognizes claim and the text as an argument.) The school should have a smoking area.

Data: (Reader asks: "What makes you say so?") Neighbors are complaining about kids smoking near the school grounds. In other schools, smoking areas have decreased complaints about smoking near school.

Warrant: (Reader asks: "So What?") The school should try to reduce neighbor's complaints.

Backing: (Reader asks: "How do you know? What makes you say so?") So neighbors will support school activities.

Reservation: (Reader asks if all counter-arguments are fairly cited.) We could increase security around the school and that would solve the problem without a smoking area.

Response: (Reader asks if response addresses reservation.) The school has no jurisdiction off of school property so we can't increase security there.

Talkback Guide for Argument

A talkback guide is a great way to get kids to notice and interpret the different features of an argument.

1. Reader asks: Does the argument report the data?

The data and evidence presented are…

    a. Reader asks: is the data persuasive? Is more information needed to establish the data? (An argument can't be advanced unless the audience accepts the data as compelling.)

    The information is persuasive/unpersuasive or sufficient/insufficient because…

2. Reader asks: Is the evidence supported and explained by warrants?

The evidence is linked to the claim by these warrants and explanations…

    a. Reader asks if the warrants are clear. Does the warrant justify the leap to the conclusion?

    The warrants are clear and convincing/unclear and unconvincing because…

3. Cites the backing for warrants, if necessary.

The backing for the warrants is/are...

  a. Reader asks if the backing supports with specifics the truth or acceptability of
  the warrant.
  The warrants are shown to be true in the form of backing that...

4. Qualifier or reservations are listed.

The reservations to the argument are...

  a. Has the arguer considered all of the objections which the audience can make
  against the claim? Have the reservations been adequately responded to?
  The reservations are adequately/inadequately addressed by...

5. Claim is cited.

What is it you should believe or do? What is it you lack? What threatens you? What is
it you need?

The claim is clearly stated as... /is implied to be...

  a. Whether the argument is convincing and why is explained. What worked and did
  not work for you as a reader? Where was the author convincing and not convincing?
  What will you do or think in the future as a result of this argument?
  I was convinced/unconvinced by the argument because... and this argument will
  inform my thinking and action in the future by...

The Ultimate Conclusion of Reading

I always conclude informational readings by asking students if they can *assimilate* the new
information and apply it to already well-established schema that they already possess (in
the case that the new information adds to but supports or abets what they already knew).
Or, I ask them, did they have to *accommodate* the new information—use the new information to make a completely new structure, or to overhaul an old one by restructuring it
(in the case when you did not know much about the topic or have been convinced that
your previous knowledge was faulty or inadequate). Another option is that students found
the new information was not new, was not compelling, or was faulty, in which case it will
be discarded.

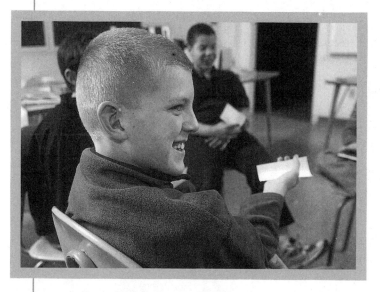

Nate offers a compelling piece of evidence as part of a debate about a fable's best moral.

As is always the case after teaching new strategies, structure reflection into your lessons—ask when students might apply this information or strategy in another text or life situation. Getting them to make those predictions and connections helps activate the strategies for possible transfer.

Jamal achieved such transfer. He recognized the higher purposes of fables and also how different kinds of writing could be used in repressive situations to work for change. To show these understandings when reflecting on our fable reading and writing, he wrote this poem:

I thought fables were just for school

But I was wrong, fables can be cool

They can help you get justice and speak what's true

And let people know what they never knew

Though it might sound strange

Fables can do your work for change

And this is hip:

you can stay out of trouble too—

If nobody knows the author was you!

CHAPTER 7

MAKING IT MEANINGFUL:
Using Think-Alouds for Performance-Based Assessment

It's fun to name your growing competence as a reader. Think-alouds show what you can do and how you are smart and accomplished as a reader and problem-solver.

After Walter made his reading activity known to me with a think-aloud, I began to point out all the expert strategies he was using as a reader. At one point, this seventh grader interrupted me and with a surprised expression dancing across his face said, "Hey, maybe I *can* get good at this!"

"Of course you can!" I replied. "You already are good at a lot of things about reading and you already *can* do a lot of things that expert readers do."

"But how come I always feel so dumb after tests and things?" he asked.

"Because the tests are dumb. Good tests should show you what you can do as well as what you need to work on. Good tests should make you feel smart!"

Our conversation continued, and I wrapped it up by naming a few strategies I felt Walter was ready to use. We set the goal for him to try one or two of these strategies during the next passage he read. Walter, usually resistant to reading, was eager to read that day and happy. We had celebrated him as a reader, and we had provided a new challenge that would help his competence grow in a visible, useful, and immediately apparent way.

This concluding chapter will show how think-alouds can be used as motivating, effective assessment tools. As I hope my exchange with Walter showed, they can be used to make strengths apparent to students and a cause for celebration. Think-alouds can also map out avenues of progress for students, displaying what they could try next— and showing how to do so in a meaningful context.

Think-Alouds: Assessing Knowledge in Performance

Think-alouds provide a performance-based assessment. They offer an in-process look at readers engaged in comprehension activity. In comparison, quizzes and tests only look at an end product of comprehension, usually only literal comprehension, and don't provide an assessment of the powerful, process-oriented meaning-making tools of readers. Tests, particularly standardized ones, also cannot hope to show the growth that occurs when students take the risk to try new strategies that they haven't quite mastered and that don't yet lead to the richest possible interpretation. Growth occurs through these kinds of risky leaps, but mastering the new strategies takes time.

As a parent, when I receive report cards on my children, it strikes me anew that grades tell us little beyond the most general impression a teacher has of a child's performance. I most value a narrative assessment that describes in specific detail what my

A Boon to Teacher Research

Because think-alouds are so effective for assessing students' reading and learning in specific ways, they are also great tools for teacher research, or more informally, assessing one's instruction. In my own teaching, I use think-alouds:

- to quickly assess students' reading on particular tasks;
- to use this feedback to inform my instructional planning: whole-class, small-group, and individual instruction;
- to see how to group kids with similar needs for specific small-group instruction; to see when to change these groups;
- to give students a way to self-assess their current situation and growth as readers;
- to help students assess each other and share appropriate strategies;
- to build student portfolios and my teaching portfolio;
- to assess student improvement over time; to get a timeline of reading improvement;
- to provide data for written assessments and comments;
- to do case studies on readers with difficulties in order to help them;
- as a teacher research tool during small classroom studies about particular kinds of reading or teaching interventions. (Please see *You Gotta BE the Book* for a description of how teacher research can work in this way.)

child has been working on, her strengths and weaknesses, ways that I can help out, and what will be worked on next in school. Think-alouds can provide the specific information necessary for writing such assessments, and think-alouds can be appended to assessments so that I can get a real flavor of what my child is doing as she reads.

As a teacher, I feel the same way. Grades, tests, and quizzes often don't teach my students much and often do not describe them very well or help me to teach them better. I much prefer performance-based assessments that will help me to do my job in a more wide-awake, wide-aware, knowledgeable, and powerful way.

Seeing improvement energizes teachers and learners. Think-alouds can show proof positive of student strategy use and progress. This kind of evidence can be used to augment other forms of assessment and replace them to some degree. Having kids keep lists of the strategies they have used, both in general and with particular texts, is a way to keep track of their growth and to remind them what they can do and should do as readers.

The following guidelines will be helpful whenever you engage in a think-aloud with a student. Refer to them as you study a think-aloud transcript, or when you talk it over with a student, or even use these guidelines to ask students to assess themselves. They will provide rich feedback and fodder for both assessment and planning. Obviously you would not use all of these at the same time; you would pick and choose the guidelines that you are helping a student to work on. What I've tried to do here is to cite a full range of strategic knowledge and expertise that think-alouds can help you to assess.

What to Watch For: Questions to Help Assess Reading

Following are some of the reading strategies and behaviors that you can assess with think-alouds:

1. **Does the reader understand her purposes for reading a particular text?**

    ____ Is the purpose personal?

    ____ Is the purpose socially significant?

    ____ Does the purpose consider a task that the reading can help to complete?

    ____ How can the reading be made more purposeful?

2. **Does the reader understand (or attempt to understand) the purposes and goals of the author?**

3. **Does the reader bring personal background knowledge to bear in understanding the text?**

    ____ What are the reader's primary sources of information about the world? about the text?

    ____ How are these sources brought to bear during the reading act?

    ____ How might the use of these information sources be expanded or assisted?

4. How well does the reader bring knowledge forward from one part of the text to another, from one text or activity to another text or activity?

____ Can the reader retell, talk back, paraphrase?

____ Can the reader make connections between different pieces of information from separate parts of the text to make inferences, see coherent patterns?

5. How well does the reader employ other general processes of reading?

____ Does the student have high expectations of print?

____ Does the student predict and verify predictions?

____ Does the reader ask questions and interrogate text?

____ What kinds of questions are asked?

____ Are question types varied to kind of text?

____ Does the reader ask inference questions? author and me questions? on-my-own or world questions?

____ Does the reader ask for help? ask stimulating questions of self and others?

____ Does the reader ask questions and make connections that help apply what is read to the real world? that transfer new processes of reading to new texts?

____ Does the reader respond emotionally?

____ Does the reader visualize settings, situations, characters of story? form mental representations of informational texts?

____ Does the student have other sensory experiences, hearing dialogue, etc.?

____ Does the reader provide evidence of comprehension monitoring? strategy adjustment?

____ Does the reader identify confusion, ask if it "makes sense," and apply fix-up strategies when needed?

____ Is reading speed varied for different situations? Does the student pause or stop and apply fix-up strategies?

____ How does the student deal with problems and frustration?

____ Are there other strategies that would be helpful to the reader?

6. How independent is the reader with a particular text or kind of text?

____ Where is the reader's ZPD?

____ Is the text easy (at the independent level)?

____ Is the text too challenging (at the frustrational level) because the reader does not have necessary background, understanding of purpose, knowledge of vocabulary, knowledge of text-type and attendant codes and strategies expected?

____ If the text is too challenging, can frontloading of content or strategy use make the text accessible in the ZPD?

____ Where are comprehension and engagement faltering?

____ At what point in a particular text is instruction and guidance necessary?

7. How well does the student understand global structures of organizing text?

____ Does the reader recognize how particular text-types serve different authorial purposes?

____ Does the reader recognize particular text-types and how they proceed from beginning to middle to end?

____ Does the reader understand and represent the different ways of presenting textual ideas (chronologically, classification, comparison-contrast, description, argument, etc.) and the uses and strengths of each?

____ Does the student understand the textual expectations (different codes and conventions, and the strategies for recognizing and interpreting these) of particular text-types?

____ Is knowledge of text structure used to improve comprehension?

____ Does the student integrate information from various parts of a text?

8. Does the student recognize text as a construction of an author?

____ How well does the reader talk back or converse with an author? How often does the reader question, agree, or disagree with an author? Does the student ever talk back to an author?

9. How well does the reader use local-level coherence to make links within sentences or to connect sentences? to link different parts of a text together?

10. How well are inference gaps recognized and inferences made?

11. **How often does the reader encounter unfamiliar words?**
    ___ What strategies are used to deal with vocabulary challenges?
    ___ What other strategies could be used?

12. **How well does the student recognize and use particular codes and conventions?**
    ___ What cues are noticed, used, and not used?
    ___ How much and what kind of guidance is needed to help the student use them?

13. **How wide a variety of strategies are used with particular texts?**
    ___ Poorer readers tend to use only one or two strategies and to use these repeatedly, even when inappropriate. If only a few strategies are used repeatedly, students can use assistance to widen repertoire and to recognize when and how new appropriate strategies may be used. Older poor readers tend to use the same strategies as better readers, but less effectively, appropriately, or flexibly. How can teaching help expand and improve on this?

14. **How well does the student learn information from text? learn ways of reading?**
    ___ How well is this transferred and applied to new situations?
    ___ How can the teacher help assist transfer?

15. **How willing is the student to take risks, go beyond the literal text, hypothesize?**
    ___ Too many text-bound comments work against active comprehension and suggest that the teacher should use interventions to foster hypothesizing, predicting, inferring, elaborating, evaluating, and conversing with author.

16. **How does the think-aloud reveal unsuspected strengths?**
    ___ How can these be celebrated and built upon?

Teacher and Student Check Sheets

Checksheets are highly adaptable—you can use them to evaluate individual readers, see patterns among students, or you can give them to students for use in evaluating themselves and each other. They can also provide great communication with parents about what you are trying to teach, how well their child is doing, and what they might do at home to help out. You can use examples like the following, design your own around specific strategies you are trying to teach, or work with your students to design ones for classroom use.

As we saw in the previous chapters, you can create check sheets or talkback prompting guides for use with specific types of tasks like inferring, reading for a main idea, or interpreting symbolism. You can also use them for general processes of reading, as we saw in Chapter 2, or to prompt and guide students to attend to the features of particular text types, as we saw in Chapter 6. Below is a variation on a general processes check sheet.

General Processes Check Sheet

Self-Evaluation	not much	sometimes	often
1. Used personal background knowledge			
2. Made predictions			
3. Corrected predictions			
4. Asked questions			
5. Used images to see			
6. Was aware of problems			
7. Used fix-ups			

As I worked with my young friend Walter throughout one school year, we often used such checksheets. At the beginning of the year he made only very limited use of the general processes of reading. By helping him to access and develop background knowledge through frontloading, and by prompting him to make and correct predictions through think-alouds and talkback guides, Walter gradually grew as a reader. We bridged from correcting predictions to monitoring comprehension and fix-up strategies. But even after a full semester of intensive work, we could see that he did not ask many questions, nor did he seem to visualize what he read.

The check sheet made it obvious to us both that Walter needed more help to visualize what he read. I therefore prompted and guided him through this process with visual protocols and other visualization techniques such as picture mapping and symbolic story representations. These techniques allowed us to "see" what Walter was able to visualize as he read and allowed us to assess and chart his progress and celebrate his considerable improvement.

THINK-ALOUD–FUELED STUDENT SELF-ASSESSMENTS

Not only do we want readers to internalize strategies but we also want them to internalize critical standards for good and engaged reading. We want them to know when they have read well and when not, as well as what to try in order to read better. It's been a core assumption of this book that if we want kids to get good at something, then we must give them the opportunity to practice it, and we must assist them in doing it. That's why self-assessment is so important: It gives kids practice in applying these critical standards, which is essential if we want them to become independent readers.

As Grist for Written Reflections

When Branwen, who struggled as a reader, wrote a self-reflection about her think-aloud of "The Chaser," she expressed: *I still pay to much attenshun to my own ideas and not enough to the story. Like when I read about the stairs I thot about how our stairs creak. But I did think about why the stairs creaked in the story, like to tell us this was scary and run-down. So I'm getting better!!! I didn't feel too much, except sorry for the girl who I never really met but no one seems to care about her. I am working on caring about people in stories, which is something I never tried before. The very sweet and bootiful end.*

Think-alouds made Branwen's strengths and weaknesses as a reader visible to her. The think-aloud process also supported her as she worked to improve her reading repertoire, and to assess her improvement, which she does here quite movingly.

At the end of the year, Walter told me: "I never knew there was so much to reading. It's kind of like it's both more complicated and easier than I thought before. I mean, it's more complicated because I didn't know all the things you have to do. But it's easier because now I know what to do and so it makes more sense to me."

My Think-Aloud Moves: A Checklist for Students

On the following page is a self-assessment checklist to give to students. Before handing it out to students, list any moves that you want them to make and monitor on the left side. In the middle, students are to check off each time they make the move. On the right, they can make comments regarding how often they make the move, when and why they made the move, questions they have, goals they want to set, and so forth.

Name _____ Date _____

My Think-Aloud Moves

Example:

Move	✓	Comments
1. Connecting life to reading		
2. Making predictions		
3. Making inferences		
a. Filling gaps		
b. Adding things together		
c. Elaborating beyond the story		
4. Visualizing		
5. Summarizing		
a. Noting key details		
b. Bringing meaning forward		
c. Thinking about the author's message		

Improving Comprehension with Think-Aloud Strategies • Scholastic Professional Books

I did one for Walter, which read like this ➔

Coding Think-Alouds

When students code their own or other students' think-aloud responses, they get into the "secret code" aspect of the endeavor—and vigorously self-assess in the process. My own pre-service teaching students have developed several different coding schemes, and I've read about several others that teachers and researchers use to great effect. So there are lots of possible variations, and you can certainly adapt or create one to fit your own purposes.

First the students do their own written or visual think-aloud, then they go back and label, or code, the kinds of moves they have made. For instance, codings for general processes of reading might be:

My Think-Aloud Moves

Move	✓	Comments
1. Connecting life to reading	✓	Use pictures from my life to see.
2. Making predictions	✓	I try to figger out what's going to happen.
3. Making inferences		figgering out how to do this.
a. Filling gaps		
b. Adding things together		
c. Elaborating beyond the story		
4. Visualizing	✓✓✓	working on this. getting good at it. Now I read and see like a comic book or seeing a movie.
5. Summarizing		
a. Noting key details	✓	I remember these things when I can picture them.
b. Bringing meaning forward	✓⁻	getting better!
c. Thinking about the author's message		hard!

PK	applied prior knowledge	AM	author-and-me question
=	connected text segment to personal lived experience	OYO	on-your-own question
V or ◐	visualized or saw something	P	predict
!	emotion of some kind	PC	prediction corrected
?	confusion	T	topic identified
(?)	asked a question	☆	key detail
RT	right-there/literal question	(☆)	direct statement of main idea or central focus
TS	think-and-search/inference question	M	comprehension-monitoring move

A few codes at a time can really go a long way, so try to use codes only for what you are focusing on with students. Invite your students to invent symbols too. Different codes can obviously be developed for general processes or for task-specific processes. Teachers can also code student think-alouds for assessment purposes. I sometimes find it useful during conferences to sit down with a student and code a think-aloud or two together.

Showing how codes for readings of similar texts change over time provides a timeline of reading improvement and progress. This can be powerful and positive for students, teachers, and parents to see.

Lifted Passages

Ask students to "lift" a short passage that gave them particular trouble from a longer reading such as a chapter. I often assign "passage lifter" as a literature circle role when we do this kind of student discussion group. Students can make copies or a transparency of the lifted passage, and the kids can examine the passage together to discuss monitoring and fix-up strategies that could be used, how what came before and after the passage would aid comprehension, how the role of prior personal and textual knowledge could be played out, and so on. I quite like this technique because admitting confusion and identifying the source of it are two important expert reading strategies that poorer readers lack.

By making the identification of trouble spots an assignment for all readers, admitting confusion becomes part of the accepted classroom project. By sharing how to attack the highlighted problems, students pool expertise, see problems they may not have encountered yet but will at some point, and are involved in an important communal activity of helping each other.

If students honestly can't find any passages that gave them trouble, then this is a tip-off that they should be reading a slightly more challenging text.

IN THE CURRENT

I often remember the joke of the accelerated reader with a chuckle. This student is proudly boasting to an adult school visitor that he is in the Accelerated Reading Program. "We really push along, we read fast. In fact," the kid proudly concludes, "I read so fast I've forgotten everything I read already!"

Sometimes we do indeed read too fast. And sometimes we teach too fast, evaluate too fast, or not at all. Think-alouds are a tool that can slow down reading, and slow down the teaching of reading, so kids get active assistance and contextualized help that can assist them to outgrow their current level of competence to become better readers, writers, and thinkers.

Good teaching takes time. If students truly struggle with particular texts and the necessary strategies for comprehending them, then it is up to us, as teachers, to teach students the strategies they need and to ensure that they get enough practice until they really know and can use the strategy. No one else will do this for the student. It's up to us. The premise behind this whole book is that what is most worth teaching are procedures. In a world where available information doubles every year, and in which the base of knowledge in a particular subject can dramatically change within a few years, learning how to learn is the most important thing to learn.

With think-alouds in your repertoire you will teach better, your kids will understand reading better, and you will both be able to name and focus on the text features and interpretive operations required to comprehend them. Students will have the assistance to actually better their reading performance with all kinds of texts, from the simple to the complex, from narrative to ironic monologue and argument. You can't get a much better recommendation than that!

Tomorrow, Jasmine and I have a challenge of our own planned. We plan to canoe in the Kenduskeag canoe race. Of course, we went tonight to check out the water flow through all the major drops. We took the time to note the river features and pointed them out to each other, rehearsing what demands each feature would place on us and how we would meet that demand. "Let's make sure to catch that black tongue at Six Mile Falls and eddy out river right in the big eddy there." "Did you see that big hole behind Split Rock! It's a keeper! We'll want to sweep around that to the left!" "If we get caught river left on Shopping Cart Falls we'll need to eddy out and ferry over to river right." We remind ourselves that one of the ways to self-correct is to backpaddle. By going slower than the current you achieve more control and have more time to make decisions. (This is precisely what think-alouds can do for readers.)

We performed our own think-alouds of our routes and strokes through every rapid. Tomorrow we'll be ready to meet the demands of the river. We'll know if something is going wrong and how to self-correct. We're confident. We're psyched. We feel competent. Ok, I'll admit it. We can't wait!

This is exactly how I want our students to feel when they approach a new and challenging reading task: with knowledge, with confidence, with a desire to successfully complete a slightly more challenging text than they have seen before and to take great pleasure in the text itself, but also with pleasure in being able to name and celebrate their own accomplishment. When they do this they will be readers. They will have moved through many zones of proximal development to the zone we call the reading zone, that place where a reader is totally absorbed in the experience of living through and conversing with the text. And what an adventure that zone can be!

BIBILIOGRAPHY

Works Cited

Applebee, A. 1993. "Literature in the Secondary School: Studies of Curriculum and Instruction in the United States." *NCTE Research Report No. 25*. Urbana, IL: National Council of Teachers of English.

Applebee, A. 1996. *Curriculum as Conversation: Transforming Traditions of Teaching and Learning*. Chicago, IL.: The University of Chicago Press.

Applebee A. 1998. "The Teaching of Literature in Programs with Reputations for Excellence in English." *Report Series 1.1.* (Albany, NY: Center for the Learning and Teaching of Literature, 1998). Microfiche.

Baumann, J. 1986. "The Direct Instruction of Main Idea Comprehension Ability." In J. F. Baumann (Ed.), *Teaching Main Idea Comprehension,* pp. 133–178. Newark, DE: International Reading Association.

Baumann, J. 1992. "Teaching Comprehension Strategies." In B.L. Hayes (Ed.), *Effective Strategies for Teaching Reading,* pp. 61-83. Needham Heights, MA: Allyn & Bacon.

Baumann, J., Jones, L. & Seifert-Kessell, N. 1993. "Monitoring reading comprehension by thinking aloud." *Instructional Resource Number 1.* Universities of Georgia and Maryland: National Reading Research Center.

Beck, McKeown, and Hamilton. 1997. *Questioning the Author.* Newark, DE: International Reading Association.

Bloom, B. 1976. *Human Characteristics and School Learning.* New York: McGraw-Hill.

Bloom, B. (Ed.). 1985. *Developing Talent in Young People.* New York: Ballantine.

Campbell, J., Voelkl, K., Donahue, P. 1998. NAEP Trends in Academic Progress. "Achievement of U.S. Students in Science, 1969 to 1996; Mathematics, 1973 to 1996; Reading, 1971 to 1996; Writing, 1984 to 1996." Washington D.C.: ED Publications.

Davey, B. 1983. "Think aloud—Modeling the Cognitive Processes of Reading Comprehension." *Journal of Reading.* v27, n1, pp. 44–47.

Edmiston, B. 1991. *What Have You Travelled? A teacher research study of structuring drama for reflection.* Unpublished doctoral dissertation, Columbus, OH: The Ohio State University.

Harvey, S. and A. Goudvis. 2000. *Strategies That Work.* Portland, ME: Stenhouse.

Heathington, B. 1979. "What to Do About Reading Motivation in Middle School." *Journal of Reading,* 22, pp. 709–713.

Hillocks, G. 1986. "The Writer's Knowledge: Theory, Research and Implications for Practice." In *The Teaching of Writing.* 85th Yearbook of the National Society for the Study of Education, eds. D. Bartholomae and A. Petrosky, pp. 71–94. Chicago: University of Chicago Press.

Hillocks, G. and M. Smith. 1988. "Sensible Sequencing: Developing Knowledge about Literature Text by Text." *English Journal* 77 (6): pp. 44–49.

Hillocks, G. 1995. *Teaching Writing as Reflective Practice.* New York: Teachers College Press.

Hillocks, G. 1999. *Ways of Thinking/Ways of Teaching.* New York: Teachers College Press.

McKenna, M., Ellsworth, R. & Kear, D. 1995. "Children's Attitudes Towards Reading: A National Survey." *Reading Research Quarterly,* 30, pp. 934–957.

National Assessment of Educational Progress. 1981. *Reading, Thinking, and Writing: Results from the 1979-80 National Assessment of Reading and Literature.* Denver: National Educational Commission of the States.

Nystrand, M. with Gamoran, A., Kachur, R., & Prendergast, C. 1997. *Opening dialogue: Understanding the dynamics of langauage and learning in the English classroom.* New York: Teachers College Press.

Pressley, M. and Afflerbach, P. 1995. *Verbal Protocols of Reading: The nature of constructively responsive reading.* Hillsdale, NJ: Lawrence Erlbaum.

Rabinowitz, P. and Smith, M. 1998. *Authorizing Readers: Resistance and Respect in the Teaching of Literature.* New York: Teachers College Press.

Raphael, T. 1982. "Question Answering Strategies for Children." *Reading Teacher* (36)2, pp. 186–190.

Shapiro, J. & White, W. 1991. "Reading Attitudes and Perceptions in Traditional and Nontraditional Reading Programs." *Reading Research and Instruction,* 30, pp. 52–66.

Smagorinsky, P. and Smith, M. 1992. "The Nature of Knowledge in Composition and Literary Understanding: A question of specificity. *Review of Educational Research.* 62, pp. 279–306.

Smith, F. 1978. *Joining the Literacy Club: Further essays into education.* Portsmouth, NH: Heinemann.

Smith, M. 1989. "Teaching the Interpretation of Irony in Poetry. Research in the *Teaching of English,* 23(3), pp. 254–272.

Smith, M. 1991. *Understanding Unreliable Narrators.* Urbana, IL: NCTE.

Smith. M. 1998. *Teaching Argument.* A workshop presented to the Maine Writing Project. July 2, 1998.

Smith, M. and Wilhelm, J. forthcoming. *Boys and Books: The role of literacy in the lives of young men.* Portsmouth, NH: Heinemann/Boynton-Cook.

Stauffer, R. 1980. *Directing the Reading-Thinking Process.* New York: Harper and Row.

Taylor, B. T., Harris, L. A., Pearson, P. D., Garcia, G. E. (1995). *Reading Difficulties, Instruction, and Assessment* (2nd ed.). New York: McGraw-Hill.

Tharp, R & Gallimore, R. 1988. *Rousing Minds to Life: Teaching, learning and schooling in social context.* Cambridge, UK: Cambridge University Press.

Wilhelm, J. 1997. *You Gotta BE the Book: Teaching engaged and reflective reading with adolescents.* New York: Teachers College Press.

Wilhelm, J. and Edmiston, B. 1998. *Imagining to Learn: Inquiry, Ethics and Integration through Drama.* Portsmouth, NH: Heinemann.

Wilhelm, J. and Friedemann, P. 1998. *Hyperlearning: Where Projects, Inquiry and Technology Meet.* York, ME: Stenhouse.

Wilhelm, J., Baker, T. and Dube, J. 2001. *Strategic Reading: Guiding Students to Lifelong Literacy.* Portsmouth, NH: Heinemann/Boynton-Cook.

Literary Works

Collier, J. 1972. *The Chaser.* In *The John Collier Reader.* New York: Alfred A. Knopf Books for Young Readers.

Hawken, P. 1993. *The Ecology of Commerce: A declaration of sustainability.* New York: HarperCollins.

Hazel, M. 1995. *Food and Feasts with the Vikings.* Parsippany, NJ: New Discovery Books.

Honey. 1996. *Don't Pat the Wombat.* New York: Knopf.

Mardsen, J. 1992. *Letters from the Inside.* London: Pan Books Limited.

Myers, W. D. 1999. *Monster.* New York: HarperCollins.

Rice. B. 2000. *Pobby and Dingan.* New York: Alfred A. Knopf.

Rylant, C. 1994. *Something Permanent.* New York: Harcourt Brace.

Skurzynski, G. 1997. *Virtual War.* New York: Aladdin.

Snicket, L. 1999. *A Series of Unfortunate Events: Book the First—A Bad Beginning.* New York: HarperCollins.

Taylor, M. 1976. *Roll of Thunder, Hear My Cry.* New York: Dial.